This book was a rollercoaster ride of emotions. Initially anger, shock and frustration at tales of insider goings on in public sector, but ultimately it leaves you uplifted, inspired and fired up to take life by the balls and LIVE! Vive la revolution!'

***Jools Riddell,** author of The Fairy Godmother Mindf*ck*

I had the absolute privilege to meet Aime on the 20th January 2023 and from that very day I warmed to her, I don't warm easily so that in itself told me what a remarkable woman she is! Little did I know what an amazing life story she had to tell too! I have felt every emotion going reading this book, I've been angry at David Oliver and wanted to punch him for Aime, I've laughed at the shenanigans I know Aime would have got up to with the Coopers and now feel proud that she asked me to be part of EMDT cohort (even if I'm crap... sorry Aime!). Aime I always remember your comment about Google and it makes me laugh and I can hear you say "Fuckety fuck fuck" and laugh! You're not a good girl you're an amazing brilliant woman and this book is one hell of a read

Sally Brady
Business Planning Specialist at Elevey Ltd

I started reading your book this aftern[illegible]

[illegible] this in [illegible] past, but the sheer extent of your work experiences are mind boggling Thank God you're one hell of a tough cookie. Knowing you from such an early age I was not in the least surprised that you had the strength to turn your life around the way you have. You have been quite right to challenge the bullies and whistle blow on public sector practices. It took courage both to act at the time, and then to write this book and I'm sure it will have a positive effect on anyone who reads it. Having read this extraordinarily positive book, I have realised how relevant it is to my life now even though I am 80 years old. I will share your book with my grandchildren and use it to help them see how individual actions can make a huge difference to your life if you are determined enough.

Rose Albrow
Lifelong Labour Activist and Feminist

It's moving. I have been amazed at the strength you have found time and time again. You are an inspiration. Your moral compass has guided you through time and time again and where most people would let it go you stood strong. It made me cry at points.
The unjustness and cruelty you endured! I love having you in my life, you bring such light wherever you go.

Jenny Cross
Marketing Consultant and CEO at Cross Productions
Entrepreneur in Residence and Pro- Vice Chancellor at De Montfort University

A Sunday morning in January 2024

9.44 am OMG Aime I've finally got round to reading the book and I can't put it down! About to make some breakfast and crack on with chapter 3.
10.51 am OK, so now I'm on chapter 12, loved my little mention. Honestly Aime I'm so fucking proud of you.
10.52 am Have you got a PR and marketing plan around your launch?
7.12 pm I have just finished the book! Aime, it's brilliant. Thank you so much for asking me to read it before launch. Can I share about it on socials?
Aime: "Oh wow, yes please!"
7.40 pm Will share a teaser tonight and a proper post tomorrow xxx [she did!]
9.30 pm Hey beautiful. Are you on Twitter? I've seen a PR request you may want? Be a great way to plug the book.

Estelle Keeber
Insta Queen, Founder, 21 x bestselling author

I'm going to buy 2 copies! One, that you sign and I can keep, and one to share amongst my family and friends. I think everyone should read this book; it is important. I was really shocked that bullying is not illegal and that such terrible things go on behind the scenes in local government. I didn't know about the Kickstart scheme, but I'm so glad this was going on during the pandemic to help young people who were out of work. Your book has inspired me to go into work several times and stick up for myself and the young people I look after. Looking forward to your author's talk in the summer at the Leek Loves Books Festival on 2nd June 2024.

Maria Smith
Leek Loves Books Festival Committee Member and Inaugural Member of The Fountain Book Club

Aime Ayrehart

Let's Face the Music and Dance

From Good Girl to Free Woman: Why I set up a Trade Union and other stories

The Employment Genie
Aime Ayrehart

purple star design

First published in Great Britain 2024 by Purple Star Publishing

Design by Clare McCabe www.purplestardesign.co.uk

ISBN13: 978-1-3999-7983-2

DISCLAIMER

To all those struggling in
employment;
I hope my book helps you
to find your way forward.

Contents

Introduction

Well, my role in living this adventure, in telling this story, is nearly done.

I am writing this part of the book last. The rest of the book is written and finished. Well as finished as I can muster right now. It is over to you.

I hope that you will enjoy the story.

I hope that you will be kind and not judge me too harshly where I have faltered.

I hope that you will know that however difficult the journey has been, it was worth it and I'm OK.

But more than this, I hope that somehow my story will resonate with your life. I hope that in some small way you may feel a little less alone, or a little more hopeful about your future.

Because ultimately, I think that we often hide the most difficult part of our lives, fearing that if we share them, we will be rejected.

But these painful, human, messy parts of our lives are actually the things we have most in common. The shared mess is something that makes us feel more human and can connect us all.

I haven't always found it easy to reach out and ask for help. Or even accept help when it has been offered.

But I hope you know that no matter how much you are worried, or struggling, or feel you have messed up; that I think you are wonderful, that you have a heart of gold and unique gifts and insights into this world that make it a better place. And I hope that you will feel strong enough to accept help from those around you, and even to ask for help when you need it. There may be lots of unkind people in the world, but there are many more kind people who will offer you a hug, and a cup of tea and a friendly ear when you need it.

Maybe you are reading this because we are friends, in which case, you can do me a solid and tell your friends about this book. It's not about the money (although hell that helps) it's about starting a revolution. A revolution of warmth, and kindness, and empathy. A world where there is less hate and blame, and more people working together with a smile and a doughnut to fix whatever needs fixing.

Maybe you don't know me at all and aren't even sure why you are reading this book. In which case I hope that you stick with me to hear my story. It would mean a lot to me.

I believe that hiding our pain and our struggles in the dark just makes them grow. So, I also hope that reading my story might spark you into telling yours. Or feeling that whilst you are in the darkness or the mud right now, maybe, just maybe tomorrow might be OK. Hell tomorrow might even end up being wonderful.

Whatever you think about my journey, my ideas, my story, I hope you will tell me about it. Love it, hate it, tell me. I want to know what you think. Maybe you will pass the book to a friend, or burn it on a fire, but either way I hope it makes you feel something. Because life is too short to feel nothing.

I want to hear your stories; I want to champion your fight. So, get in touch, whether you want to tell me about your wins, or your struggles. And who knows, maybe we will become great friends, or maybe I can help you, or someone I know can help you. If I can be of service, that would make me very happy.

The world is a mess right now.

But together, I think.

Well, I think we got this...

Aime Ayrehart

The Employment Genie

PART ONE:
I decide to make a stand

Chapter 1
An unexpected wakeup call

I had persuaded myself I didn't really need counselling. I was just the person commissioning the service. But to commission the service well, surely, I needed to test that the provision was good, didn't I? Strangely over my HR career, I've done this several times. So obviously I didn't really need any help, I was just you know, doing my due diligence.

There was a crisp autumn feel to the air that day. I don't like to be late, so I arrived early and parked. The counsellor worked from home in a beautiful, listed building at the end of a country lane in Northamptonshire. I felt slightly guilty as I was visiting during work time, I had so much to do. I parked the car a little way from the house as I had a few minutes, and I wasn't sure exactly where it was. The low sun felt nice on my face and helped me bury any thoughts that I might actually need this session, those feelings were far too messy and uncomfortable, and that was a Pandora's box I was not ready to open. Or so I thought.

Do you believe in fate, or journeys or destiny or karma? I wasn't sure, I'm still not sure, but I do know that sometimes things just seem to happen when you are screaming for them. As the counsellor opened the door, I felt welcomed and safe and sank into the comfortable chair in her beautiful library with a deep sigh.

I didn't really notice when the questions went from small talk about the lovely weather to questions about me. And then she asked a question that shocked me to my core and changed my life.

She asked what I did for fun.

Still half thinking about the report I had to write tomorrow, and whether I'd remembered to buy this year's book day costumes or send out the party invites for my daughter's birthday party, I didn't really notice the question.

A talkative person who will fill my own and other people's discomfort with a stream of language I was stumped.

Fun?

I didn't answer.

I played with the word in my head a little, but there was no connection. I couldn't really understand it. It felt like a foreign word, an alien word, a word that somewhere deep inside my brain I should really understand what it meant, but I just couldn't quite recall its meaning.

In my silence the counsellor opened a file and pulled out a single A4 page entitled "Fun" and handed it to me.

It was a list of things people enjoyed. She asked me to read the list and tell me which of these sounded like fun, which I enjoyed doing. I read down the list:

Bowling

Dinner with friends

Going for a walk

Sport

The list went on.

Well obviously, not sport, that has never been fun for a bookworm like me.

She asked me when I last remembered having fun?

Fuck.

Fuck.

Fuckity fuck fuck fuck.

I couldn't remember.

She asked when I had last been playful?

What me? Playful?

Was that something I did I wondered? Again it seemed alien.

"Would you like to do some of these things for fun Aime?" she said again, kindly, well ahead of me on the curve of what the fuck was going on here.

How the hell had this happened?

I vaguely remembered the notion of fun and play, but they seemed like things I had done decades ago. I was almost 40, in fact I was due to turn 40 in a few months.

And finally, after what seemed like an eternity, I remembered I love rollercoasters, and sunshine and my family. There was something there, a spark, a hope, a distant memory of a time when I wasn't so buried with work and parenting and adulting, so focused on everyone else's needs that I had forgotten I was even a person, let alone a woman who liked to play.

I left the session in shock.

I was due to go back to the office, I had three missed calls on my phone, and dozens of urgent emails.

I walked slowly away from the house and lent against the fence looking into a field. I couldn't catch my breath, I felt numb, I couldn't even cry.

But deep deep down, somewhere in the depths of my being, a long-forgotten voice stirred.

The voice of a person who remembered fun, and who I was, before I was smothered and drowned and blocked and underestimated and mocked. It was like a tiny spark, a candle, within the darkness. It had never gone out, it had just been forgotten, shut away in a dark corner gathering dust and cobwebs.

But although small and buried, it was resilient and feisty, it had not gone out no matter how dark it had got.

And that day I suddenly noticed it again, and it burnt just a little bit brighter.

This is my story of what happened next. It was painful and exhausting but also exhilarating and unexpected. It has led me to places and situations I could never have thought possible. But however tough it has been, I'm still glad I found that spark again.

And if you can walk through my story with me, through the challenges, the problems, the darkness, you will find that this story has a happy ending.

Chapter 2

I decide to fight for my life - whatever it costs, whatever it takes

It is Saturday 23rd September 2023 as I sit writing this. I am now 46. I am sitting at my desk in my pyjamas in Leek Staffordshire. My feet are cold, and I could really do with a cup of tea, but I need to write this.

I've been putting this moment off, and even now I'm not sure I have the strength to tell my tale. I've learnt many things over the last few years, and one thing is that once my subconscious has decided I'm going to do something, then there is no point trying to fight it.

This was a story I needed to tell.

Mostly because I hope that writing it will be cathartic, that trying to find the words will be a way of making sense of the journey. It is time to move onto the next stage of my life, and to do that I need to come to peace with what has happened.

Burying my feelings, the pain, the discomfort, has not been a healthy thing for me, and I'm slowly learning to open that Pandora's box and deal with what comes out, whatever it might be.

But it feels like I am a toddler learning to walk, stumbling, confused, which seems at odds against the professional, capable facade I have maintained for so long.

But no, that is unfair, it isn't exactly a facade.

That is me, it is just one part of me, the tough, resilient, adulting part that has enabled me to do things that frankly most other people wouldn't even try.

But I have ignored other parts of me, for too long.

Yes, I'm stalling, whirling around not quite ready to be this vulnerable and open.

Because I know that it isn't just about writing the words (however painful that is).

I'm actually scared of my words being read.

Because although I have a strong core, and I am comfortable with who I am, of course I care what other people think. Not everyone, but there are some people I really care about what they think, friends, family. And well if I truly tell them how I feel, will they be angry with me? Will they think less of me?

As I write these words, the logical part of me, the part that is a scientist at heart, the part that has a clipboard and a white coat and understands hypotheses and split testing. That part of me is reminding me that the evidence appears to be, that not everyone hates me, and that people do get something sometimes about what I write and say. I'm not for everyone, but there are people reading these words wondering what happened next that might find the story of my journey useful.

But I need to stop stalling, my feet are getting cold, and I've promised myself that I won't get up until I've written through this bit.

So here goes.

This is where my story starts.

You see that tiny spark I remembered that day in the counsellor's office, wasn't just my sense of fun, it was also my resilience, my survival, my desire to be and exist and be seen and be myself. And without realising it, I had made a decision that day.

I could not bear to merely exist grey and lost and adulting.

I had decided I was going to fight.

Fight for something ephemeral and existential that I wasn't even sure that I was allowed or should fight for.

I was going to fight to be me.

I was going to fight to have joy in my life.

I was going to fight for my opinion and my right to have a voice.

And well, I was going to fight to live not just exist, no matter how hard the fight, no matter how painful, no matter who hated me or got angry at me.

And with each thought that flame grew a little.

Alone and still buried, some of the cobwebs were brushed away and it was a little stronger.

Before the story was over it would become a raging fire and nearly destroy me, but we are still at the beginning of my tale.

But it wasn't just the "fun" comment that had shocked me during that one counselling session.

"Do you realise that what he is doing isn't OK Aime?"

"Do you realise that he is frightened of what you are capable of?"

"Do you realise that it's not just you he's doing it to, but you might just be the only one strong enough to make a stand and change things?"

"Do you realise that it isn't your fault, that you are doing a great job?"

"Do you realise you are good enough?"

Huh?

What was going on here?

Seriously, what the fuck? I'm not a victim, I wouldn't let people treat me badly.

I am tough, I am strong, I am confident.

But then it began to dawn on me. I was tough, but I still swallowed the Kool Aid.

I hadn't heard of the phrase the "good girl" then, that is something I learnt later as I started to unfurl all of this junk and conditioning in my head, examine it, consider what was actually useful and replace it with better ideas.

I had been talking about my job. I had been talking about my boss, David Oliver, the Chief Executive of East Northamptonshire Council.

I saw him as a nice guy, a good guy. He blamed me for everything that went wrong, and well I was supposed to be the expert and really good with people, so if something went wrong it was clearly all my fault, wasn't it? If he got angry at me, it was my fault because I had said something he didn't like. If he shouted at me or ridiculed me that was because on some level I deserved it, didn't I? I just wasn't good enough, I need to try harder, learn more, be better, then I would be accepted, then I would be good enough?

Oh dear. It is painful writing this. How could I ever have been so dumb? So blind? So conned? But I have also learnt to try to be kind to myself. A fish does not see the water it swims in, it knows only water. And we all accept the realities we have absorbed. That does not make me stupid, it just makes me like everyone else, human. Yes, I have some skills, but I am still flawed. But I know something now that I didn't know then.

I am good enough.

On my worst days, when I've messed everything up (or feel that I have), when all I can do is drag myself out of bed and make a cup of tea, I am still good enough.

But I hadn't got there yet.

It took a little while for me to process it. To process what I had learnt that autumn day. Then all at once I knew what to do. I had had enough, and I was going to do the one thing, no one ever thought I would do.

I was going to speak up.

And I was going to keep going, no matter how many people tried to shut me up, no matter how much money I was offered to keep quiet, no matter how much I was threatened (and I knew all of that was coming, I might not have known exactly how and from what direction, but I knew it was coming).

I'm not sure that I could have done it if it was just for me, but I realised that it wasn't just about me. There is sometimes a moment, when the thinking moves from "Why me?" To "If not me, then who else?" And I realised that if I didn't do it, then nobody else was going to.

So I went into the office that Monday morning and wrote three emails.

1. I put in an equal pay claim.
2. I became a whistleblower.
3. I put in a bullying and harassment claim against the Chief Executive of a local authority.

Strangely calm, I then went about my job.

But of course, I had unleashed a hurricane. Because the last thing these men wanted me to do was tell the truth. Because, well I knew what they had done, and I knew where the bodies were buried.

They were scared of me for a reason. Not because I'm inherently a scary person. But because they knew what they had done, what they were doing, was wrong. And they knew that I was the one person who would be able to put all the pieces together. And they thought I might just be the person who might tell the truth, whatever it cost me.

It wasn't me that was scary, it was the truth. The truths that they had been burying and covering up. The things that they were ashamed of.

Chapter 3
How not to run elections

There were three things that David Oliver, the Chief Executive of East Northamptonshire Council (ENC) was ashamed of.

Things he would have preferred I hadn't noticed.

But I'm afraid I'm the kind of woman that notices things, and when I find a problem, I want to try and fix it. And when he realised I had noticed, he and his cronies did everything they could to make sure that I kept quiet. I mean there were obviously more than just three things, but well, if I tried to write everything down, I'd be here for a decade, so let's just focus on these three problems.

1. Elections at ENC were run terribly.
2. There was a toxic culture of bullying that stemmed from the top.
3. Men were routinely and consistently paid better than women.

When I got the job at East Northamptonshire Council (ENC), one of the attractions was how small an organisation it was, whilst still being complex. With slightly less than 200 staff, and a small senior management team of about 20 staff, give or take, it meant it would be possible to get involved in a variety of things, get to know people, but with all the complexity of a local authority.

I also liked the job itself.

I had come from the NHS where I was Head of HR Shared Services and Head of Learning and Development (a common thing when someone is capable, and there are two vacancies, well why not just give both jobs to the same person - so much cheaper!). I was managing a team of 50, a budget of £7 million, a combined payroll of almost £100 million and supporting 10,000 staff across seven NHS organisations. But whilst I loved the work that sitting at this level of such a large organisation allowed, I missed rolling my sleeves up and getting work done myself. I had teams and managers who delivered services, and they had a tendency to feel undermined if the boss suddenly actually wanted to do some interviews, or plan out a whole training programme, or even possibly deliver some of it. And I didn't want to upset them or undermine them, so I stayed in my office and did the strategic thing and senior manager stuff like a good girl.

But the role at ENC covered everything up and down and across. I would be dealing with the strategic work and advising the Board and the Leader of the Council, but I only had a team of three, so I needed to do some of the actual work too. And if it hadn't been for the way that I was treated, and the way other people were treated, I would have been like a pig in shit for the rest of my career, loving every minute of it. But whilst my team were fabulous, and we built up a great little culture between us in our corner of the council, outside our little bit it wasn't so nice.

Elections were one of the things that I was curious about. I'd worked in Social Services, Education and Corporate Services the last time I'd been in Local Government, so I hadn't got to learn about Elections.

I like to understand how things work, so when I started the job, obviously I needed to understand what the processes were, and who did what. Things were difficult from the very first time I met the Elections Manager, let's call her Alice shall we.

She was evasive when I asked her simple questions, like how much are people paid (pretty important as I oversaw payroll, and it is pretty darned impossible to check that it is being done correctly if you don't actually know what correctly looks like). She didn't want to tell me. I couldn't quite understand what was going on. Was I being thick? Was I upsetting her somehow? Was there some aspect of this that I was just missing? Why wouldn't she tell me how much people were paid?

Of course, there was a reason she was being evasive. She didn't want me to know what was going on, because that might very well land her in jail. But I of course didn't know that at the time. She evaded me, re-arranging meetings, saying she didn't have time to explain anything to me (there was always an emergency, and you know like I didn't want my curiosity to delay an election so, well that seemed fair).

So, I left it and got on with everything else I needed to do. David Oliver seemed happy with the way Elections ran, so I didn't have it on my list of things that were a complete and utter disaster and needed fixing (and it was always a long list) so I just got on with my job.

That was until the day an election went very very wrong.

I knew an election was going on, because it's all over the news and everything, but I didn't really have anything to do with the running of the election at ENC at that point. It was a complex election with lots going on. ENC wasn't one of those places where we try to get all the votes counted in two hours, so that the election would finish, and the votes would be counted through the night and then we would announce usually by about lunch time'ish the next day.

When I got to work that morning, I had an urgent message to go to the chamber of the council. Odd I thought, but OK. I wandered down, naively wondering what might be going on.

I walked into a shit storm.

Alice had a lovely project plan for the election, and she had been reporting to David every week with lots of green ticks to say everything was done. But it was all a lie. The elections process had gotten severely behind but she didn't want to admit it and just did that thing where you blindly hope that you will get back on track.

I walked into the room and there were papers, envelopes and ballot boxes everywhere, seemingly in a jumbled mess. Alice and the deputy elections manager had walked out and given up in the middle of the night because it was all fucked up and they didn't know what to do about it. David Oliver, as the Chief Executive, was in charge, but nowhere to be seen, and apparently no-one could find him.

What the fuck?

I mean seriously what the fuck?

I think my family has a particular trait, probably genetic, and it is the opposite of panic. My brother and sister both have actual medals for bravery for things like running into burning buildings to save people off duty and you know catching bad guys and stuff. But anyway, when things go really astray, we all just get calm, and just start sorting things.

And this is what happened to me that morning. It didn't occur to me until much later that we would have been all over the news if anyone had actually seen what was going on. At that moment there was a job to do, we had to get these votes counted, we needed the job to be done properly, and somehow in very little time, not knowing what the fuck we were doing and then David would need to stand on the podium and read out the results.

I wasn't the only person who had been called into that room that day. So, we worked together, someone said "Aime you're pretty good at excel", well yes, kind of, I'm no expert but I can find my way around it.

"The verifying spreadsheet was never created, can you create one?".

OK, so what the fuck is a verifying spreadsheet I wondered? In the next 84 minutes I learnt what one was, and created one the best I could.

If you are wondering, it is a document that compares how many people are eligible in a ward to vote, how many people are registered in a ward to vote, against how many votes have been cast during the election, with checks for things like, how many votes were submitted by post, and how many at each voting station and each ballot box. It is meant to check for fraud, it should make it impossible for example to just squeeze a fake ballot box into the room with fake votes and pretend that they were submitted (because of course each actual voting slip has nothing on it about who you voted for, so once it is out of the box you haven't got a fucking clue where it came from). OK, it was a two cherry Pepsi Max job, but I got it done, tested the formulas and figured, well it would have to do. Right, now to start putting the numbers in.

I looked up, there were piles of paper everywhere, half opened envelopes, and a busy but slightly panicky feeling in the room. As I watched things going into rubbish bins, I was a little worried about some votes being not counted, but in the situation trusted the other managers in the room, after all they probably knew more about this whole mess than I did even if they weren't in elections either.

OK, so let's start with the postal votes I thought.

Now postal votes start coming in long before the actual election day. And on that lovely project management spreadsheet Alice had been happily reporting that they had been counted each day as they came in and logged, only that was complete bollocks. The problem was at this point that we weren't quite sure what had been counted already.

I'd seen elections on TV before, I'd even attended counts, and this didn't look like anything I had ever seen before. For a start, usually there were candidates and their representatives checking and watching what was going on. You know those TV pictures on the BBC of sports halls full of tables of people counting ballots and people walking round checking that no one is pocketing ballot papers or adding anything in. I never did exactly work out why it all went quite so wrong, or why we were sitting out of sight in a room with no monitors, but it had been a complex election, with lots of people voting on lots of different things, including a referendum, and I guess TV doesn't always show the whole picture does it. Whilst yes there was a room somewhere with people doing that, we still had a part to play.

So, we got it done, the best we could. We got all the postal votes counted, and verified what we could. The outcomes were announced a little late but not by too much. I didn't go to the announcement, but I heard later that it all went broadly as expected with one small hiccup.

One of the local candidates who lost, quietly went up to David after the election and suggested that whilst he had always known he was going to lose, that the numbers announced for his ward couldn't have been quite right, because David had read out that the winning candidate had received more votes than there were people to vote...

A couple of days later I was summoned to David's office, and we had a crisis meeting about what to do to make sure this didn't happen again. I assumed I was being called because we were going to be sacking Alice, but no.

David didn't want to sack Alice, despite the monumental fuck up that had happened. Sometimes my inside thoughts can be seen on my face, and I think at that moment David was pretty clear I was thinking "why the fuck not" (by the way I don't actually swear at work, or in front of my mum (she was a primary school teacher and still doesn't like it) but fuck it this is my book, and I swear a lot in my head, and fundamentally this is just me typing what is in my head so yes there is likely to be a lot of swearing, and I'm not even going to bloody well apologise for it (and do you know how much therapy it has taken to get to that point 😂😂😂).

Anyway, I probably actually said something like "really, and why would that be?" Attempting to say it in my calmest, politest most professional soft non-confrontational voice (a voice which of course all good girls must adopt at all times, except maybe occasionally in the bedroom when men seem to like other voices...).

Basically, David didn't want us to sack Alice because the Elections Commission would probably ask questions, and he didn't want the Elections Commission to ask questions, so Alice was staying, but of course we still needed to fix elections.

"So Aime, we need to create a new role, something that will be about helping managers to re-design processes, such as elections but not just elections. Can you create a job description and person specification, and an advert, and recruit someone like that for us, but we haven't got much of a budget so you're going to have to find savings elsewhere, oh and by the way can you start the work on elections right now, and just you know cover things and make sure things go OK while we get this person".

Oh, you are fucking kidding me. So not only is this bloody woman staying, but I've got to try and fix this mess, behind the scenes, with no money, until I can recruit someone who can take over?

There are pretty much two ways to deal with this kind of situation. Abject despair or roll your sleeves up and give it ago. I mean I do like doing unusual things, and I had wanted to find out more about elections, and well I have trained multiple people on things like business process re-engineering and lean and project management. I've re-designed numerous complex public sector systems behind the scenes, so elections? Why not? If I'm honest, I did actually quite enjoy stepping in to help sort out how elections were run.

As messy as that day had been, it was to get much much worse though, because, I hadn't even discovered the fraud yet.

Alice and her team, still in situ, were of course not exactly impressed with my involvement. But I started by splitting the task up into largely three parts:

1. Recruiting this new role - because a great person in the job would then be able to sort out the rest of the shit.

2. What was urgent and needed sorting before we got the new person in post.

3. The actual bit that was my job - I needed to understand how the pay worked and the money was being given out, because at this point, I was beginning to realise that what I thought might just be someone vaguely avoiding me might be more sinister, a lot more sinister.

We sorted number one and got a fabulous appointee who did an amazing job and I learnt loads from and really enjoyed working with him.

Number two was a bit hairy at points, but we got through. You know your polling cards, those little slips of paper that get sent out to you before an election? Well, we needed to get some of those out before the new guy started. At this point I was running the project management and I needed to approve the printing of 30,000 of these and I'd been given the proof. Now I have some skills. Proof reading is not one of them. I read for meaning, my grammar is shocking, and I can't spell for toffee. Fortunately spellcheck resolves most of these, but you can't spell check 30,000 individual polling cards, and names and addresses plus actually the errors are likely to be missing something that is needed, not spelling something wrong. I spent several hours trying to find someone who knew what they should say and was better at proof checking than me. But no one was around, the deadline was now.

So, I took a deep breath.

And I had to do it myself.

Fuckity fuck fuck fuck.

Fortunately, it was the one time I did actually manage to proof it properly, I picked up one small mistake, confirmed the change with the printers and we were good to go. But that was scarier for me than speaking in front of ten thousand people.

OK, so one and two sorted, right, now to look at the money.

Whilst Alice was still incredibly wary of me, she had started to realise that she wasn't going to be able to avoid me, and that evasion was probably actually a bad strategy.

I hate that people are sometimes wary of me (although I can understand why to some degree). I only ever want things to work and people to be happy. If that could happen and I could solve interesting problems and watch sci-fi on TV and hang out with friends, and sleep in late, and eat too much, then I'd be happy as Larry. I remember watching a Simpson's episode where someone threatens Homer saying he will take away everything he enjoys about life. Homer starts to panic, and Marge just turns to him and says something like "Homer, your greatest pleasures are drinking beer, watching TV and not having to get up early at the weekend, I think the greatest evil mastermind in the world would probably struggle to take that away from you, you're safe". At which point Homer is reassured and gets on with his day and the evil genius gets very frustrated. I am a bit like Homer, it is hard to destroy me and take everything I enjoy away, when what I like is so simple.

Anyway, I've digressed. What was I talking about?

Ah yes, I hate people being scared of me. I think some people get a kick out of it, but I usually go into overdrive to try and explain why they shouldn't be scared of me, and or trying to reassure them that I am kind and nice and not trying to hurt them. But of course, I was missing the point. People aren't actually scared of me. This isn't about me, it is about them. They are scared of something, being found out, being not good enough, being judged, disappointing someone. And I scare them because I sometimes seem to them like the person who might see through them or notice their mistake or be disappointed.

In some ways them feeling threatened by me is probably some kind of backhanded compliment. I once had someone say to me in anger "well you think you know everything don't you Aime". I thought about that for a while. Knowing everything, well if we considered not just all knowledge currently understood by every human, or recorded in every book, but also every piece of knowledge that might be possible to know, including everything we don't yet understand, then quite frankly everything is a lot. Then comparing what I know with that. Then my knowledge is incomplete, biased, and skewed and quite frankly infinitesimally small when compared to what could be known. So of course, I don't know everything, in fact if we were to round my knowledge, it would round to zero, it would be easier to say I think I know nothing than I know everything. So that statement doesn't really make any logical sense.

And then one day, still thinking about this reaction of people to me, which is distressing and confusing, I had a lightbulb moment.

They didn't really think I thought I knew everything, they thought I was suggesting that I knew more than they did, or that I was right, and they were wrong, and that this made them feel something. I'm not exactly sure what, but it wasn't pleasant for them.

Oh, and explaining that I didn't think I knew everything because of the vastness of knowledge, wasn't helping.

And anyway, this was about them not me.

So now I just try to smile. Or try to explain my theory on messing things up, and how we are all flawed, but that is OK, and that I am more flawed than they could possibly imagine, but so is everyone else, I don't think I'm better than anyone else because we are all the same. But I digressed, again seriously, so right where were we.

Ah yes, Alice decided that it was easier to try to be nice to me than to keep hiding. We sat down and I said, right, just talk me through how the salaries work for elections.

There are two groups of staff that work on elections. A small team of full-time staff who are on typical council salaries, and this includes the chief executive (so David Oliver) who is the Returning Officer or deputy returning officer[1] (although the CEO has other duties and the elections team don't). This group is then supplemented by around 200 casual staff who work for a day or two around the election (these are the people who run the voting stations).

I needed to find out how all of these people were paid and how much. It turned out that Alice was running a separate payroll, unchecked by HR, finance or audit, for all the additional payments. She was manually creating payslips and calculating tax. The full-time staff had their normal salaries paid through the main payroll (which I ran) but it was just their bonuses that were paid by her manually.

Sorry, what bonuses?

We don't pay bonuses in local authorities.

I mean the pay is crap, but at least we all know it is usually crap for everyone, so it seems fair right? We can all moan that we can't afford anything together.

"What bonuses are you talking about?"

She went pale, but I think she realised that she was going to have to tell me. Or maybe she was at that point where she just thought it would be a burden lifted.

"Well, I write the bonus cheques for David, me and my team, and then sign all except my own, which David signs."

What?

So, you mean you write a cheque for David's bonus, and yours and then you sign his and he signs yours and you swap them?

Yes.

And what about tax.

"Well, we don't need to pay tax on them".

What the fuck is going on here...

And who approves these payments?

"Well, I said, we do, I sign David's and he signs mine".

But what about elected councillors and audit and finance and payroll?

"Well, this is the way it's always been done, no one has ever had a problem with it before".

And so how much are these cheques. "Well usually David gets around £10,000 per election and I get about £5,000 and my team each get a few thousand for each election".

"So, it's not going through payroll, it's not being taxed, it's not being approved, it's off the books, and its tens of thousands of pounds, how on earth has this not been picked up before? Surely audit would not be happy about this?" I asked.

"Well David approves the audit scope each year, and it doesn't include elections because they are different. We have a different bank account, which David and I oversee, so well it's none of Audit's business".

It's not often that I am truly lost for words...

At this point you might be thinking, well bloody public sector, it's all useless, I'm not surprised, or perhaps you are thinking the opposite and are feeling defensive, "well people do their best" or even perhaps a little ashamed.

After a brief flirtation with the private sector after University (I worked in book retail for Books etc and Borders UK) I have worked in the public sector for most of my professional career, mostly in the NHS and public sector, specifically Mental Health Trusts and Social Services. And I have met and worked with some of the most AMAZING public sector workers. I have worked with people trying to fix things, and people putting their heart and soul into serving and helping people. I've also come across so much deep despair, and that is just the staff, desperately trying to make sense of, work within and help from a system that is completely broken.

Quite rightly the public, you, me, everyone demands a service fitting of the people and needs they have, keeping us safe, keeping us healthy, educating our children, organising our elections. But years and years of under investment mean that the services are held together with string and duct tape and computer systems that are 20 years old. And staff are passionate and caring but broken and exhausted and on strike because they can't afford to pay their mortgages or feed their children. But everyone is too tired to feel any empathy for anyone else, and if not in full burnout then right on the edge.

And by the way I appreciate it isn't any easier in the private sector or running a business or being young or retired. It is difficult trying to make money right now, it always has been, shareholders expecting growth every single month irrespective of the market and small businesses struggling to deal with rising costs. And even those people that seem to have it all, the glamorous and rich and beautiful and famous, are sitting at home at night desperately trying to hide the deep insecurities that led them to need the fame and are hungry because they've been on a diet for their whole life.

So, everyone is struggling, all the time, and blame, well I'm not sure that blame helps. But we do need accountability, and it isn't all gloom. No matter how bad everything is, there are beautiful sunrises and sunsets, birthdays and new love, coffee, long chats with friends, walking barefoot in the grass and of course doughnuts.

But back to our story of the elections. Because of course the solution isn't anger or blame, it is to roll up my sleeves and see how I can help fix the problem in front of me. It isn't great, but it is fixable. So, I create another to do list:

1. Work out how much everyone is getting paid and write a schedule.
2. Get the payments approved properly.
3. Move the elections payroll onto the normal payroll system so that it is taxed and audited properly.

ENC head office was a beautiful, listed building set in the countryside. One sunny autumn morning I brought coffees and doughnuts to the Democratic Services Manager as it was going to be a long day.

Every council meeting is minuted, and historically the minutes go into big leather-bound books called the minute books. Older versions of these that went back to the council's first month, were stored in the safe, which was a beautiful old room with a heavy safe door like you would imagine would be in an old bank. The room itself was strangely beautiful. Whilst most of the historic features of the building's past, the glorious fireplaces, tiles and floors had long been covered up with some designer's idea in the 70s of what was modern. And apparently modern meant ugly and cheap. But in some corners, like the safe, where nobody had bothered to modernise there were gorgeous little forgotten walls of ancient glossy tiles in vibrant greens. We dug out the minute books and went backwards. We were trying to find the original authorisations for the elections payments and teams. Surely, we thought, there must be some minutes somewhere. As the day drew on and the doughnuts and coffee depleted, and our bodies began to ache from sitting on the floor, we escaped the building to sit outside on the bench in the sunshine overlooking the fields next to the glorious flowers that a lovely member of staff had planted.

"Well, we've gone back 20 years and can't find anything except a very old generic approval for payments to be in line with the national guidance, what now?".

We fixed it by writing a new paper. We worked together and looked at all the current payments and compared them with national and local standards. Made recommendations, put it through consultation and all the necessary approvals, talked to Cabinet Members and David Oliver, and the Leader and Deputy Leader of the Council (elected posts) and created what we call a pink paper. A paper for a council meeting that is highly confidential (they really were printed on pink paper). Then we talked to all the people who organised the various levels of meetings and took it through the committees and sub-committees all the way up to full council. We sat in the Council Chamber ready to present the paper and deal with any questions from Elected Councillors and Members, but after all the work, and with some trepidation about what questions we might get asked, the elected officials approved it without discussion, their attention for the evening was focused on how much it should really cost to get rid of a rat infestation.

Days and days of work and planning and thinking and sorting, to fix a problem that should never have happened, but it was done, and well of course we ate more doughnuts. I sat on the bench watching the evening sun set at around nine o'clock (council meetings are in the evenings after a full day's work) and ate my doughnut with some degree of satisfaction, before the hour-long drive home, where hopefully I would get to see my kids before they were asleep.

But the story of the elections does not end there. You see, once we had gone through that whole process and realised that the elections team were getting huge bonuses, that weren't defensible. They were removed, and guess who the team blamed?

But I told you there was fraud, and well although dodgy, what had happened so far was murky and unfair but not necessarily fraud. The thing that could and probably should have sent Alice to jail hadn't yet come to light.

As well as being the elections manager, Alice was also a Magistrate. For about 25 days a year she would go and sit in the magistrates' court instead of coming to work. The agreement was that the council would release her, to help the courts system, but that on the days she worked for the magistrate she would be paid by the courts not us.

One day one of my fabulous, amazing, HR team put their head round my office door...

"Aime, Alice wants me to sign this form for her but I'm not sure I should, can I show you please?"

"Of course, come in, let's have a look"

The form was from the Magistrates court, we needed to sign to say that we had been deducting a days' pay from Alice's salary each day that she went to the Magistrate's court. Signing the form meant that they would release her Magistrate's salary payments for those days. David usually signed the form for Alice, but he was on holiday, and she needed it in a rush, so she'd come into HR.

"She just said I should sign it, but I thought I'd better ask you"

Great team mine, good instincts!

"Well check that we've made the deductions, and then sign away" I said, secretly pleased that they were checking things properly!

I forgot about it for a few days and then the team member came back, and popped her head around the door again, this time with a cup of tea in my favourite mug and a chocolate biscuit, she looked slightly worried.

"Aime, you know that form Alice wanted me to sign, she's been hassling me and chasing it, but I've found a bit of a problem".

Now the approach, as you might have guessed by now in the team, was that if we hit a problem, we rolled our sleeves up and fixed what we could, working with the fabulous colleagues in the building. And if there was a mistake, whether we made it or someone else our mantra was "Fix it, learn from it, move on" because well life is too short for blame and recriminations and there are always new problems to fix.

But this had something a little more worrying attached... fixing this looked like it was going to be painful.

"Well, the problem Aime, is that we have never made any deductions".

I thought about that for a moment,

"So have we been paying her AND the magistrates have been paying her for the same days?"

"Yes, and it goes back years and it gets worse..."

Worse I thought, oh joy of joys like I didn't have a thousand other things to do today anyway.

"Well, I checked our system, and Alice has been taking sick days with us and then going to work on those days for the Magistrates office".

Oh crap, this was going to be fun. A magistrate has been committing fraud that has been signed off hopefully accidentally by the Chief Executive because he probably just trusted her.

I have run million pound payrolls, and have been audited within an inch of my life my whole career, but I have also been the person who tends to get called to do the really difficult messy complicated politically sensitive disciplinary investigations. I have sat and sorted through documents and records to uncover numerous frauds in public sector organisations, worked with the police and counter fraud teams. I've also investigated hideous accusations of child abuse, elder abuse and sexual harassment.

I knew how to deal with this kind of investigation.

Over the next few weeks, after informing all the authorities, including the Magistrate's court, and working with a fabulous ENC internal investigator whose day job was investigating issues to do with potential fraud around benefits claims, we got to the bottom of the matter.

Our investigations suggested that for years Alice had been double claiming for her work. She had been claiming double pay for the days she worked at the Magistrate's office and getting David to sign off to say that she had had the money deducted. The amount of money she had unfairly claimed was thousands of pounds. And that was on top of all those lovely bonuses he had also been signing off that hadn't gone through payroll properly or been audited.

Now every council has its own internal processes for dealing with fraud, generally we end up dealing with benefits frauds etc rather than staff. And the policy at ENC was that if the amount received or claimed unfairly (as sometimes people did this accidentally not realising for example that having their boyfriend come and stay four nights a week meant they were entitled to less housing benefit) was over £2,000 then we would seek a criminal conviction.

Our investigation done we had to report back to the Chief Executive (David Oliver) and the Magistrates court. We had written our report and compiled our evidence and both agreed it was pretty clear that she had inappropriately claimed the money.

In the interview she had suggested she did it accidentally, that she just wasn't good with admin (which after the elections fiasco I quite believed). Personally, I didn't believe it was entirely that innocent, but it wasn't for me to decide what happened to her, we just did the investigation.

I arranged a meeting with a senior person at the Magistrates' court, and then something truly shocking happened. I explained what had happened, and that were likely to need to dismiss and perhaps that there needed to be consideration of a criminal investigation. The officer at the court said

"Well, we have a problem".

Apparently, the courts had assumed that all its magistrates, fine upstanding honourable people that they were, had always been honest with their requests for payments, so none of the expense's requests had been checked as carefully as perhaps they should have been. They rarely even checked that the magistrate had been in court the day they claimed for, let alone that the appropriate deductions and been made elsewhere. But modernising their systems had led to numerous errors being discovered. I wondered what they were going to do, and she suggested that the people high up were worried that the truth would undermine the public's trust in the court system, and enrage them as it was unjust (the magistrates having given people at times what those accused felt were draconian fines and even prison sentences for what many of those convicted felt were small misdemeanours). So, what were they going to do I wondered? Was this one of those things that was going to be all over the news and the subject of a Channel 4 documentary? No, they were just quietly going to ask those magistrates to retire, including Alice and do nothing.

I sat quietly mulling over the unfairness of the matter, seething if I'm honest.

I think my team suggested I go for a walk (their usual and kind and healthy suggestion when I looked like I might actually explode) so I did... and then walked back and got on with my day job. This was not something I could fix, no matter how much I wanted to.

Then we arranged a disciplinary hearing for Alice, and warned her that she could well get dismissed. She stormed into my office shouting, telling me I'd got it all wrong, then burst into tears and said she hadn't meant to do it and it was all just a big misunderstanding, and then started shouting at me and threatened to get a lawyer involved.

Yes, please get a lawyer involved Alice, because a lawyer would quickly realise just how much trouble Alice was actually in.

Which is exactly what happened. I got an urgent phone call from her lawyer the next day. Would we accept a resignation?

You see in public sector organisations, we have some slightly different disciplinary policy clauses. If someone does something that is considered damaging to the public, we continue to investigate and hold a disciplinary hearing even if someone resigns. It is intended to stop someone simply moving on and committing fraud in another public sector organisation or abusing children in a different school, resigning every time they get caught, but never actually being dismissed. The lawyer knew that this could lead to a criminal conviction and dismissal, and was negotiating but with a somewhat pleading tone, she had seen the report and the evidence, she knew that her client was in incredibly murky waters. But this wasn't my decision to make, it was the Chief Executive's.

Can you guess what happened next?

"Just let her go quietly Aime, we don't want the Electoral Commission breathing down our necks, now do we, just let it go, we won't bother to have a disciplinary hearing". So, with a heavy heart and feeling that this was really not how this story should end, but at least that Alice was leaving, and hopefully therefore that the carnage would stop, I rang her lawyer who was overjoyed. I suspect she went back to Alice crowing about her amazing negotiating skills, never really appreciating that this was much bigger than her.

I raised concerns about how elections were run at East Northamptonshire Council as part of my Whistleblowing allegations (remember, one of the three emails I sent were Whistleblowing allegations). But David Oliver and the Conservative Councillors did not want my allegations to be investigated, so they tried to ignore my allegations.

Most councils have internal finance teams. They then pay one of the large consultancy firms to be internal auditors to check that they have done things correctly and to recommend any amendments to processes. Councils work closely with both internal audit and their finance teams. Then when everything is done, a separate accountancy firm come in and do an external audit. This is much tougher and much more independent and there are strict processes and procedures that are required to be followed.

With it looking like no investigation into my whistleblowing allegations regarding elections was ever going to be done, I went directly to the external auditors. They were not happy that no investigation had been done, and independently appointed a legal team to investigate my allegations. Their report was produced in January 2021 three years after I had originally raised my concerns.

In the executive summary of the whistleblowing investigation, it was confirmed that

"We found that the majority of the allegations were potentially valid whistleblowing allegations."[2]

The report acknowledged that, and I quote

"It is clear that the Returning Officer [David Oliver] was aware that there were deficiencies in the running of the election in question." [3]

And...

"It is not in dispute that allegations of fraud were raised against the Electoral Services Manager, in relation to them falsely claiming sums they were not entitled to from a third party and from ENC in connection to her role with the third party. ESM resigned before the allegations were considered under a formal disciplinary procedure and ultimately no findings regarding their culpability were reached."[4]

The whistleblowing investigation report was then delivered to Conservative Councillors at ENC.

Without a meeting, they decided that neither themselves or

David Oliver had done anything wrong, and it was concluded that no action was necessary.

Was I angry?

No not really. I was just exhausted. I had done everything that I could. I had cleaned up the elections, got them back on track, and reported my concerns to the correct authorities. If they then wanted to just ignore the report, well then, I guess the only thing left would be to write a book and let you the readers decide whether this is how you feel your elections should be run...

Chapter 4
Bullying at ENC

I'm not an easy person to Bully, but David Oliver still found a way. But I wasn't alone, plenty of people were being bullied at ENC.

Bullying is an insidious practice, and perfectly legal at work. In fact, most people, especially when they contact me via the Trade Union, are surprised that there are absolutely no laws that force organisations to treat you with respect at work or ensure that there is no bullying.

Most of employment law is based on contract law. You can sue for unfair dismissal. You can also sue for discrimination on the grounds of one of the nine protected characteristics covered in the Equality Act 2010 (list). But you can't sue for being treated appallingly. You can leave and sue for constructive dismissal, but it is almost impossible to prove, and most organisations are quite keen that people go, so they will take the risk and know they will rarely lose in court, and if they do they won't lose much money.

Most people think that if they do win at an Employment Tribunal, they will get big money. But most of the time employers win at Employment Tribunal. Despite the occasional big payout to an ex-banker, most employees, even when they do win at Employment Tribunals, don't win much. Thank you to Innes Clerk (Morton Fraser) for his annual table of the compensation awards on LinkedIn (saves me looking up the actual research!).

For April 2022 to March 2023

The most commonly awarded amount of compensation awarded for unfair dismissal was £6,201 (the median if we are getting mathematically technical for the stats people out there), and the average (the mean - add all the awards together and divide the amount of money between the number of awards) gives you the grand total of £11,914.

Bearing in mind that you don't get legal costs in an employment tribunal, and that it is likely to cost you at least £10,000 in legal fees to go all the way through to an employment tribunal, this means that even if you win you are probably going to end up out of pocket.

Awards for discrimination are higher, but last year the most common award for sex discrimination was £11,177 and disability discrimination £15,643 - so you have still probably made a loss when you've factored in your legal costs.

There are only two winners in the employment law system; employers and lawyers.

Employment law might seem like it protects the employee. It doesn't, it has no teeth. This is a shock to most people. But well, as a Trade Union there are still things we can do, and well by now, you've probably worked out that I am a bit of a sucker for a David and Goliath fight!

But we were talking about bullying weren't we.

There is no legal definition of bullying, because it isn't actionable in court, and isn't defined in law, so there is no need to define it.

ACAS[5] describes bullying as unwanted behaviour that is either:

1. Offensive, intimidating, malicious or insulting
2. An abuse or misuse of power that undermines, humiliates, or causes physical or emotional harm to someone.

It goes on to state that bullying might:

- Be a regular pattern of behaviour or a one-off incident
- Happen face to face, on social medial, in emails or calls
- Happen at work or in other work-related situations
- Not always be obvious or noticed by others

They state that "it can still be bullying even if they do not realise it or do not intend to bully someone"

As I said, I'm not an easy person to bully. I can remember three attempts at school, all of which backfired in one way or another.

The first was when I moved primary schools from Staffordshire to East London. I was eight and the new school was an austere Victorian building with concrete playgrounds but no grass at all. To get from the front playground to the middle playground there was a narrow alley between the school building and a 10ft wall that marked the edge of the school grounds. The alley was only about six foot wide, and was long. It was the only way during playtime to walk between the playgrounds.

One day, when I'd only been at the new school a few weeks I got caught walking between the playgrounds, completely out of sight of any adults. I didn't have any friends yet, so no social protection. It was just me. A boy in my class squared up to me, surrounded by his mates. A few other children stopped playing marbles (seriously we did actually still play marbles, I'm old!) and started to watch. Pre videos and iPhones at a time when there were only four channels on the TV kids had to get their entertainment mostly in the real world.

The boy started to say nasty things to me. Why had I come here, I was ugly and fat and looked like a boy (I had very short, cropped hair at the time - far more practical than long hair if you are playing).

The bully expected me to cry, or get upset, or maybe even wet myself.

Instinct took over.

I walked up to him and punched him in the face with every ounce of my strength.

It was the first, and only time, I have ever hit anyone.

His nose started to bleed, and he looked at me.

He saw the look on my face and realised that I was not scared of him. And that I would probably keep hitting him, and even though I was a girl, I would probably fight dirty.

His instincts took over, and he ran. I thought he might get a teacher, but he was too embarrassed. Nobody ever tried to bully me at that school ever again. I made friends and really enjoyed primary school.

The next time someone tried to bully me I was at secondary school. I think I was in the first year (or year 7 in new money). I was the only person from my primary school who had gone to Coopers, so I didn't know anyone, and again I found myself having to make friends from scratch.

I got a strange phone call one night. I didn't really understand it at all. I didn't really think much of it when I went in the next day. I found out later that it was a prank. Someone had got their big brother to pretend to be a famous radio presenter and to act out a scenario where the radio presenter rang me at home to play some sort of game that would be recorded and if I won, I would be on the radio. I think I was supposed to go into school all excited and tell everyone I was going to be on the radio, only for someone to embarrass me to explain it was all a hoax. I never listened to the radio, and I had no idea about popular culture (I was the nerd sitting in the corner reading a book, I was not a popular kid at school and never even vaguely cool - in fact I was the complete opposite of cool). I had never heard of this radio show, or the set up, so well the bullying attempt backfired totally. The bullies were again starved of their joy in my distress, because well I hadn't understood or got distressed.

The only other time I remember someone trying to bully me at school was in the sixth form (year 12 and 13 - in new money). I was a school captain, and that gave us a few responsibilities and we actually had a little office, although it was shared with all the sports captains, and although I was fencing captain, again, totally uncool. I sat somewhere we called the dead zone, where all the weird people sat. I don't think I ever once sat in the main common room where the popular kids sat, in fact I'm not even sure I went in there except once or twice. But I wasn't really bothered. I liked the kids in the dead zone. And didn't much like the popular kids.

We all had lockers, and one lunchtime one of the sports captains said they had found a key but they didn't know whose it was, would I find out?

Of course - I was happy to help (I was always the Good Girl, I volunteered a lot at school and was awarded the service to the school prize in both the upper and lower sixth, after winning all the main academic prizes and several individual subject prizes lower down the school, I was also fencing captain, competed on the Maths team and helped my best friend organise the sixth form music events - you get the picture...)

Eyeing up the locker room, I worked up a systematic plan of action to go through the lockers to find which one it worked for. It took about 20 minutes and I found the right locker. I went back to the person who had asked and said it was locker two three eight five or whatever, and he burst out laughing, as did his friends, and said.

"We know".

I didn't really understand until later what they had done.

In the moment I just said

"Thank you, I really enjoyed that, a very calming way to spend a little time" and happy as Larry walked off.

You see I had found the whole situation very zen, or in today's parlance mindful. I had enjoyed a simple repetitive problem to solve amidst the stresses of a seventeen-year-olds life. And I hadn't understood that they had tricked me and tried to embarrass me, so I wasn't upset.

You see bullies get a kick out of upsetting and humiliating their victims. And, I don't react like most people, so they don't get the high they are after. So generally, they just leave me alone.

I feel for bullies. People copy what they have experienced. You'd think that once someone had experienced poor treatment then they would never want anyone else to, and this is the case occasionally. Unfortunately, all too often they merely become the very thing they hated. It is all about feeling powerful. Feeling powerless is a horrible feeling. You feel scared and vulnerable with no avenue to turn. If someone is belittling you, or humiliating you, or hitting you, or just neglecting your needs, especially if that someone is someone who should be looking after you, it is a terribly powerless feeling. But then the bully can feel powerful by doing the same to someone else, in front of witnesses, and suddenly they aren't powerless anymore.

Bullies are not happy, confident, well-adjusted people. They hurt other people because they are already hurting, and they just want to feel a bit better. It is no excuse, but I guess I feel sorry for them. And of course, that is why they hate me, because I don't give them what they want emotionally, partly accidentally.

But David Oliver was a bright man, and he had the time and the desire to work out just how to find the gaps in my armour so he could upset me and feel powerful.

A question people often think when people (especially women) are treated badly by men is why don't you just leave? This is a complicated question, with no easy answer, but for me I think it has two answers:

1. You genuinely believe that it won't be better elsewhere, that whatever is happening will just be repeated again in another organisation, and that not having a job is risky, and that another job will be worse.
2. Bullying can be very insidious, especially where it includes gaslighting and groups of people ganging up on you. You can end up believing it is all your fault, that you deserve the treatment, that you are no good. It is hard to leave and get another job because that requires confidence, the very thing that has been eroded.

Until relatively recently I did think all the bad behaviour I had experienced throughout my career had all been my fault. And don't get me wrong, I'm no angel and there is learning for me too, but and I'm going to say this slowly.

It was not my fault I was badly treated.

I did not deserve it.

I worked hard, was good at my job, did my best, was kind and understanding and loyal.

It was not my fault.

There, that feels better.

The first day David Oliver, the Chief Executive of East Northamptonshire Council, became my line manager, he said "You'll be pleased to hear that I have a poor memory, so if you ask me something one day and I say no, don't worry, just ask me the day after and I'll probably say yes" and he laughed thinking this made him the best boss in the universe.

What the living fuck?

So basically, absolutely no clarity, ever.

Because it didn't always work that way round. Sometimes he would say yes, then forget and say no later. Oh, and he was completely happy to do it in public and say something like "well actually Aime I know you might think that is a great idea, but I don't" - despite the fact he had asked me to do it the day before...

And he wanted to believe he knew HR better than me, but struggled to remember the stuff, so even if I prepped him before a meeting, he would often forget, and then blame me for not prepping him properly.

Feeling psychologically safe is important to everyone at work, and I didn't feel safe. I did my best to stay away from him as much as possible. I also avoided being alone with him after a particularly uncomfortable situation.

We had been interviewing all day. Whilst I mostly just went to work with my hair in a bun and no make-up, and dressed pretty casually (it was a council where people don't generally dress that smartly) it was an interview and so I'd made an effort. My hair was down, I had make-up on and a smart dress. The interviews had finished and we were just discussing the next days' interviews and I guess we were just chatting, he had walked back to sit at his desk and I was kind of leaning/perching against it and then he called me by his wife's name...

I pretty much ran out of there, and he got annoyed. In a one-to-one soon after that he told me that I wasn't allowed to leave a meeting in which he was present, without his permission.

He made me feel trapped, and he loved that. He also knew that I knew that refusing to follow a direct order without due cause was insubordination. But this chapter isn't just about me, it is also about how endemic bullying and harassment were at ENC.

In 2017 I was asked by David to undertake a stress survey. Sickness levels had been rising, and to be honest I think he genuinely wanted to understand what was going on. But I think he also thought that people would just talk about overwork. I used the Health and Safety Executive's guidance on what creates stress in organisations to compile a survey. I don't think David looked at the questions carefully before it went out, he thought he was such an amazing leader that I don't think it ever occurred to him that we might be opening Pandora's box.

People were very stressed but it was the results on harassment and bullying that were most shocking:

25% of staff said that they had been harassed by elected members.

30% of staff said that they had been harassed by colleagues or managers.

12% of staff said they had been bullied by colleagues

And 10 % of staff said that they had been bullied by their manager

In addition to this in regards to support:

23% of staff felt they were never or seldom supported by the corporate management team

And 11% felt that they were never of seldom supported by their managers

There were some open-ended questions for feedback at the end of the survey, these got very personal, and were excluded from the report. In fact the corporate management team felt that they were so damaging they were never shared.

The results made uncomfortable reading, and David and the Leader of the council didn't really want to deal with the root cause, or admit that there was a problem. In the forward to the report setting out the statistics above, David and the Leader wrote

"We have consistently received positive feedback from you about what a good place this is to work and we need and welcome your involvement in making it better. We don't want to focus on stress - that feels like a "glass half empty" approach. We want to focus on improving employee health and wellbeing... we encourage you to take the advice of Mind...connect, be active, take notice, learn and give".

Fundamentally they didn't want to tackle the issues. It was easier to just tell staff that they needed to exercise more. The report was not shared widely, and wasn't followed up.

To be fair, it's not really surprising in hindsight that the culture was as it is.

East Northamptonshire Council was an almost overwhelmingly Conservative run council for its entire existence, with only one or two Labour councillor's elected out of 50. The local MP was Peter Bone. The Leader of the Council worked closely with him, and he was considered to be one of the leading voices for the Council.

As I write this, Peter Bone is currently suspended from parliament for bullying and sexual misconduct . The complainant who was a member of Peter Bone's staff (who hasn't been named but who initially complained to the Conservative Party in 2017 about Peter Bone's behaviour but was ignored (sound familiar?)). Having been ignored, the employee complained to the Independent Complaints and Grievance Scheme at the House of Commons. An independent expert panel recommended Peter Bone's suspension from parliament after finding that:

"Mr Peter Bone MP committed many varied acts of bullying and one act of sexual misconduct".[6] The report states that on a work trip with an employee he "dropped his towel and exposed his genitals close to his employees face when they were in the bathroom". The report also states that MP Peter Bone repeatedly hit and verbally abused the young male member of staff, and frequently asked him for massages. In conclusion it stated he had "verbally belittled, ridiculed, abused and humiliated" [7] the employee.

The suspension has triggered an automatic recall petition and a by-election.

Nice bloke, great example to set...

Is it any wonder then that the local conservative party was rotten when they had such lovely leadership?

I've already talked about the issues that I had in relation to David Oliver and elections at East Northamptonshire Council. It is fair to say that by the election in April 2018 things were quite tense between David and I around elections.

I was away in the run up to the election, I took an extended holiday to go to Florida. We had a new elections manager by then, but without me in the building the team still had a tendency to revert to old habits. One ongoing issue we had was about ID checks.

It is a legal requirement for every UK employer to check that an employee has the right to work in the UK.

As a local authority we had been contacted by the Police Counter Fraud team who had asked to deliver a course to staff on the vital role of public sector ID checks in making it much harder for gangs to legitimise organised crime including drugs, human trafficking and child prostitution. People tend to trust that someone who has a job (or had a job) with the council, has probably been checked properly.

It is important to check that people are who they say they are, otherwise, we might be employing people who do not have the correct qualifications, or are using a fake identity, or are hiding from arrest for criminal allegations of violent crimes.[8]

When those checks go wrong, the wrong people can get into positions where they put the public at risk. Ian Huntley had a criminal conviction for burglary and numerous criminal allegations for sex offences against children. But when he applied for the role of caretaker at Soham Village College the background checks weren't done properly, and two young girls ended up being murdered.[9] The Headteacher stated that if he'd known about the burglary conviction, he would not have appointed Huntley...

And I don't know about you, but I don't want it to be easy for criminals, and people who might be working for foreign states to get access to our ballot boxes. I'm a pretty easy going and open-minded person, but I'm not naive enough to think that other states or connected services might not have a go at messing with our elections if they thought they could get away with it...

You might think that I'm being a little extreme here. But an ID check only takes a few minutes and is easy to do. It isn't painful or upsetting to the member of staff. I will happily personally check thousands of ID's to make sure that the one person who is a bit dodgy, doesn't get anywhere near our ballot boxes or our children.

Because an ID check only gets done once at a local authority, when you apply for your first job and go on our system. We very rarely check ID again, so once you are in, even temporarily, then you can apply for other jobs, without further checks.[10]

I'm a pretty pragmatic non-rulesy kind of person. But some laws and rules are just sensible. I don't drink and drive, and I make my children wear seatbelts. And at work, I make sure ID checks are done on employees. Now no system is perfect, but you need a system.

The elections team had taken advantage of my being on holiday and ducked my team and avoided doing ID checks on elections staff. We had a nice system, when casual elections staff turned up for their mandatory training, we did ID checks. Nice and easy, no one has to come into the office specially, and we get everyone done all at once. But they hadn't done this. When I got back, me and my team were trying to get the ID checks done bit by bit, but the elections team still didn't like doing it. So, they complained to David Oliver. The rule was, they don't get on the IT system (and therefore paid) until their ID check is done. They didn't want to have to do this, they just wanted them paid anyway. But I knew that once people were on the system and paid, it was going to be very difficult to go back and do ID checks. Getting paid is a pretty good motivator to get people to adhere to something as boring as an ID check.

The fine for not doing an ID check for someone who doesn't have the right to work in the UK is £20,000 per failure and can lead to a jail sentence of up to five years.[11] There aren't many things specifically to do with HR that you can go to jail for... this is one of them.

In June 2017, getting fed up with this rule, the elections manager went to David Oliver to see if she could get him to override my process and get the remaining elections staff on payroll without ID checks. I had said no, because I knew it would be slippery slope, if we let some on, next time we wouldn't get any ID checks done for elections staff... he agreed that elections could ignore me, and the elections manager wrote to David to get this in writing.

29th June 2017[12]

To David Oliver and Aime Armstrong

Subject Staff Payments

Morning David,

As per our conversation on Tuesday can you please re-confirm that you wish all staff that worked for the NCC and local elections in May to be paid asap.

Many thanks

X

29th June 2017

To X, Payroll Manager and Aime Armstrong

Dear X

Yes, I can confirm that: I want anyone who has not yet been paid for the county Council and local elections to be paid immediately. I understand that there is still some confusion about what ID is required in order to confirm that they are eligible to work in the UK, but I would like to remind everyone that I am the employer for that election, not ENC, and I am willing to take the risk rather than have people wait for months to get paid, which I do not consider to be acceptable.

I gather that the same issue may result in people getting

paid late for the General Election. Norman Stronach is the employer in this case so his instructions need to be followed, but again, people should be paid without delay.

Regards

David.

I took this as a direct instruction to just get the remaining staff on the system without the ID checks, which I was very worried about, I took some time to word my response, but it is as follows:

29th June 2017

Hi David,

I do agree that we should get everyone paid as quickly as possible, and will endeavour to ensure this will happen. We have almost everyone appropriately ID'd (I think we may only have a handful that are not now). Unbeknownst to me, elections decided to take over this aspect of the elections process without the proper understanding of what was needed in terms of paperwork. They were also then too busy to meet with my team or myself when we tried to help them by explaining what was needed, and cancelled meetings when they were booked. With better planning, organisation and communication there is no need for elections payments to be anything other than efficient and streamlined albeit it will always be a resource intensive process getting so many people paid appropriately.

I am not prepared to breach the right to work ID requirements (which are strict and specific) nor to ask my team to do so. It would be a breach of my professional and ethical responsibility both to this council and as Member of the CIPD, not to mention a breach of the law. It could open yourself, this Council and the election process itself to significant legal financial and repetitional risks, especially in relation to the change in the law that was implemented last summer.

It is inappropriate of you to ask me to ignore this rules, and if you continue to insist that myself or my team should do so, I shall use the protection of the whistleblowing policy and legislation to raise my concerns.

Again, I totally agree that once all this is over, we can sit down and work out how we can make this process easy and clear for everyone, and again, I'm happy for my team to take on the paperwork aspect entirely, as long as we have a name and contact details before the action election. Or, I'm happy to talk through what is needed, and for elections to continue to undertake this role. As you are no doubt aware, HMRC have changed a number of rules around elections payroll. We have successfully implemented all of these changes, it is much tougher and more hassle now, but there is no way back I'm afraid...

Regards

Aime

David was furious with my response. He summoned me to his office and shouted at me for what seemed like ages. He told me that I'd better just learn to do what I was told or he would get rid of me. I was under no doubt that he meant that I needed to do what he told me to, or he would sack me.

I put in my complaints instead.

It took me ages to get ENC to investigate my allegations of bullying. I had to contact the external auditors again. I also think that me submitting an employment tribunal claim had an impact.

Eventually, an external investigator was appointed. The Barrister who undertook the investigation into David Oliver bullying me concluded[13]

"When asked whether he spoke to AA in a threatening way, David Oliver (DO) admitted that he "may have raised his voice as I was very frustrated and I felt that AA was being deliberately obstructive" but denied that he was threatening towards AA.

Instead DO felt that AA had been threatening towards him by "threatening" whistleblowing and "exaggerating the potential consequence of any breach in his situation".

DO felt that "AA had taken a 'jobsworth' attitude."

The Barrister went on to say "Having considered the correspondence, I do not agree with DO that AA's email of 29th June was "aggressive and threatening".

"I consider that AA was entitled to raise her concerns, which appear to have been genuinely held, regarding the payment of workers and the right to work checks. As further explained by AA the Home Office guidance in respect of right to work checks has civil and criminal penalties. I consider this to be a serious matter and do not think that it was unreasonable for AA to raise her concerns in the way that she did."

"DO was, by his own admission, frustrated at AA's response. I find on the balance of probabilities that DO did shout at AA and that his behaviour would have been perceived by AA as threatening and intimidating and that it undermined her confidence and self-esteem. Whilst I appreciate that senior officers in organisations do need to be able to have frank, honest and challenging conversations. DO was clearly in a position of senior to AA and I do not consider that it was acceptable or justifiable for DO to raise his voice at AA in these circumstances..."

The investigating Barrister concluded her bullying investigation report with the following paragraph[15]:

"I do find that there were some occasions where DO's behaviour fell below the professional standard expected of him due to his own frustrations and that, in hindsight, he ought to have conducted himself more professionally and been more mindful of the impact that his behaviour may have on other employees, especially coming from a position of seniority".

The report went to a committee of Conservative Elected Councillors at East Northamptonshire Council, and they concluded that there had been no bullying or inappropriate behaviour by David Oliver.

Again, I could have been angry. But I wasn't, I was just disappointed. Even with an independent external investigation by a barrister concluding that David Oliver's behaviour was unacceptable, the local Conservative councillors merely decided that in their opinion David Oliver was allowed to behave as he did, and that there would be no consequences for him. There is a pattern emerging here...

But East Northamptonshire Council weren't just annoyed with me about raising bullying concerns about myself, they were also annoyed about me for following due process about investigating other bullies.

One day, I was sitting in my office, and a member of staff, let's call her Penelope, came into my office in tears, seven months pregnant, with her coat on and with her bag. She had already had a tough year. I'd been liaising with the police to keep her safe because she had been targeted by a jealous ex of her partner. It was suspected the partner's ex had not only put dog shit through her letter box but had also firebombed her car (which was destroyed but fortunately no-one was hurt). The threats to her life were real, and we had a number of processes in place to keep her safe at work and safe getting from home to work. Her original boss had been made redundant in staffing cuts, and a colleague had started getting very involved in her role which she felt was bullying behaviour. After talking through a strategy with the senior manager overseeing the areas, I interviewed the colleague C with their manager M.

C was not happy about being interviewed about a potential bullying grievance. In fact she got very angry. She felt that Penelope wasn't performing well at work, and she was angry that her manager M wasn't disciplining Penelope. She felt that she should never have been interviewed about her behaviour. In my disciplinary hearing (more on that later) I was accused of being too pro staff. In this case, it was suggested that I had been heavy handed during this interview.

Here are some quotes from a personal statement the colleague made following the informal interview about her behaviour towards Penelope.

"M told me I had a meeting with him and Aime in HR to discuss what Penelope had spoken to Aime about…M said to a member of staff that there was going to be a bucket load of shit flying around, or words to that effect…"

I was furious when I found out that the line manager had set the meeting up like that. Informal investigation meetings like this are meant to be as relaxed as possible. There is no assumption of any fault at this point, they are just exploratory. But if the manager tells the person being interviewed that "a bucket load of shit is going to be flying around" then that is likely to make them defensive, upset and worried before they even enter the room. It can be almost impossible to then run the meeting in an informal and relaxed way.

"Aime said she just wanted a chat. I immediately asked her what Penelope had said. She said she wasn't going to tell me. She then asked me how do I feel things are in the team? I said up until Thursday lunchtime I would have said fine. We chat, laugh, she jokes, discuss home life, etc. Aime said well that's not how Penelope sees it. You could have knocked me down with a feather. M never said anything in confirming or denying what I had said. Aime asked me why I was getting upset and I said it's because I feel disappointed that Penelope didn't speak to me. She said it's no wonder if I had the attitude I came across to Penelope as angry... I said several times I am cross, upset and angry because of her questioning me, when I haven't done anything wrong…I asked Aime what does she want me to do, just ignore errors? She said, no you can't do that. That's when the errors are given to M. She kept putting words in my mouth trying to say I was looking/checking for errors. Several times I said I wasn't and hadn't. I did confirm D had asked me to check her work and feedback to her and D spoke to Penelope each time. I said I have copies of many of mine and D's emails about errors, she wasn't interested…She (Aime) would not accept she was making me cross and angry as I am not that type of person…Each time I mentioned I know Penelope can do the jobs as she gets some right on all levels she has been trained on, but she doesn't stay focused and concentrating (because she is on her mobile phone all day long). She said that's my perception and I cannot say that. I said it's not my perception I can see. I mentioned D has mentioned her using her phone too much and needs to keep off it. I have emails to prove this. Aime wasn't interested…I told Aime it became very clear almost immediately that Penelope couldn't do the work they had been lead to believe…Aime kept saying throughout I can see your angry and upset, very condescendingly. She was the one that was making me cross and angry. Aime said Penelope had lots of stress in her life - I said haven't we all. Aime said very condescendingly - if there is anything we can do to help. I said sort this two-year-old issue out … Aime said just because you may work at a very fast pace doesn't mean everyone can. I said I did not say that. This was because I mentioned how little work she gets through. When I mentioned the latest list of errors which has sparked this issue, I asked M [the manager of both of them] if he had looked at each one. He said that no he hadn't. I couldn't believe it."

From time to time, people get fixated about whether or not a colleague is working enough, or getting things wrong. The employee here shouted at us for more than an hour, angry and frustrated that management had not dealt with this member of staff in the way that she had expected. It was not surprising that anyone might feel bullied by this person, her tone was aggressive, her manner accusatory. She was totally unaware of her own behaviour, or that it was inappropriate to continually badger a colleague about perceived mistakes when their manager had not chosen to act on it.

What the colleague would never have known is that my impression was that this whole situation was being handled poorly by management. A layer of management had been taken out, and that had clearly led to an issue in the team, but rather than deal with one employee's concerns about another's, management had done nothing, possibly even inflamed the situation. The colleague had felt they weren't being listened to and had continued to tell the employee that their work wasn't good enough and that they shouldn't be on their phone. The employee had felt bullied. The manager had then inflamed the situation further by setting what was meant to be an informal meeting up to be some sort of inquisition.

This whole situation was a failure of management, and a breakdown of relationships that had got out of hand. By the time it had got to me, one employee was feeling bullied and the other was feeling that they were being attacked because an allegation of bullying was being investigated. It was quite a mess.

David Oliver and Glenn Hammons (you'll find out more about him in later chapters), apparently believed that this entire situation was my fault. They didn't seem to have the empathy or emotional intelligence to understand that if someone is told before a meeting by their manager that they are going to be in trouble, and that a trip to HR is framed somehow as being sent to the Headmaster's office to be told off, then no matter how supportive or caring I am, it is an uphill struggle to get them to believe that I'm not out to get them.

But again, well, you can't win them all, but in this case, I did get a rather nice email out of the blue a few months ago from Penelope. She had searched for me on the internet and found my company email. She said the following...

> Hi Aime,
>
> I don't know if you remember me, but I worked at East Northants Council at the same time as you. I was pregnant and experiencing severe bullying and I came to you off the cuff after being humiliated for the final time in the middle of the office and you very kindly told me to go home and rest and protect my unborn baby. That day I started bleeding through stress. As a person with O negative blood any bleed is a risk and requires a trip to the hospital for an anti d injection.
>
> I was so touched that day as you were the only friendly face, I had experienced in what had been a very difficult few years on the receiving end of indirect and direct bullying.
>
> When I eventually came back to work, I had been told you were not available and I was not allowed to contact you. The bullying continued. The humiliation continued and eventually in November 2019 I handed my notice in to start a job back in Corby council in December 2019.
>
> Penelope

The culture at ENC was not a healthy one. I did my best to try to both create a healthy one and help senior managers and the elected councillors to understand that the example they set was key, and that a healthy culture where people are treated with respect, and conflict and issues at work (which always arise) are dealt with appropriately and with care and tact.

I felt like a failure at the time, because I hadn't fixed it, and people hadn't understood me, but now I just see it as an uphill struggle, that one lone voice (however loud I spoke) was not going to change the tide. I did my best...

Bullying may not be illegal, but I think it should be. We now have legislation that makes it a crime to emotionally abuse a partner. I think we should have a law that says we should not be bullied at work. I don't think it should be criminal, but I do think employees should be able to go to an employment tribunal. I think it is time that bullies at work realised that we aren't going to accept this kind of behaviour anymore. But I don't think it is about destroying the bullies either. They are usually hurting and damaged in some way. I think it should be more about getting them to empathise with the pain they are causing and try to seek some help for their own pain. I am not looking for vengeance, I am looking for solutions that help everyone.

Chapter 5
How women got paid less at ENC than men.

When I started at ENC I noticed a team of casual workers were listed as being employed in what we called Revs and Bens. This stands for revenues and benefits. Revenue basically means council tax. This was the part of the council that keeps the records and deals with all the issues around collecting your council tax. They work out who should pay what, issue the demands, and check who has paid, then they deal with changes and people who ask for their money back. There is a lot of data and a lot of paperwork and a lot of letters sent out from this department. There were around 13,500 households to write to and deal with.[16]

Casual workers are quite common in any organisation, so initially I didn't think much of it. It also made sense that Revs might have some.

ENC had a large number of contracted out services, this meant that there were less than 200 staff who actually worked for the council and were paid by the council on the payroll. So over time, whilst I didn't know everyone, I learnt about every role and team.

After a few years, I realised that for a casual workers team there hadn't been much movement in the team.

Payroll is a more complex process than most people realise. It requires a large amount of small changes to be made every month. I have spent a lot of my career, commissioning, and running payrolls. Each month the payroll and the HR team each made some changes to the database. They did things like adding new starters, sorting out expenses, calculate sick pay and maternity pay, and calculate changes of hours, changes of salaries and leavers. When we say that payroll has been run, this is actually pressing a button and allowing the system to analyse all the information and calculate everyone's tax, NI and pension, and then create a pay slip for each employee, and a list of payments to be made by the finance team. Payments aren't made automatically, an individual finance officer makes the actual payments from a list (once these have been appropriately signed off). Or for larger payrolls the list is submitted to the bank who then makes the payments. Then various reports are created, one is sent to HMRC, one is sent to the finance team and incorporated into the finances of the organisation (payroll in public sector organisations is usually between 70 and 85% of the total budget), then a final report is sent to the pension providers. There is a moment between running payroll, and sending out all of the payments and reports, when errors need to be checked. To ensure that there is no fraud, there is always a separation between the people who can make changes on the system, and the person who verifies the run. This is to stop the person doing the verification creating what is called a ghost employee (an employee who gets paid but doesn't exist, the money going straight to the fraudster). It was my responsibility to be the person who checked the payroll before the payments were made. To do this I ran a variety of reports that I had personally created. There are standard errors I'm looking for - very large payments and very small payments being two of those (the rest, well you don't expect me to give away all my secrets, do you?)

But issues with this team weren't coming up in my payroll checks because I wasn't looking for consistency, in fact I was looking for problems.

What I did next opened a massive can of worms. You see I'm a naturally curious person, so when I get what I call an "itch" I tend to follow them.

I got an itch about the casual team, why hadn't I seen more movement in the payroll reports? I would expect to see new starters and leavers in this team if they were genuinely casual workers. So I got an itch, and followed where it went...

At this point I was in the process of shifting all our paperwork into digital formats. I'd created new processes and new systems, but we still had a backlog of old files that hadn't been uploaded. I went and got out the paper files of the individuals in the "casual's" team.

I wanted to find out how long they had been with the council. I expected to find out that it had been months, possibly a year or two.

The actual answer shocked me.

So how many years do you think that the longest casual worker had been with the Council?

Go on, think of a number before you turn the page to find out the answer.

42 years

WTF?

That was a shock.

They had started straight from school in their teens, and worked for their entire career at East Northamptonshire Council, and were nearing retirement.

Not exactly casual then.

Then I realised what this meant.

You see, any person employed as a "casual worker" at ENC was treated differently in terms of their employment.

The presumption was that they were on a zero-hours contract, could be offered work, but could also turn it down.

Zero-hour contracts have been contentious for years.

They are legal but can be hugely detrimental to staff as they often get short notice about how much work they can get and may not be entitled to things like company pensions.

One thing that most managers don't understand is that a contract isn't just a document that you get at the beginning of your employment. In employment law a contract is much bigger than that one document and is made up of the following:

- The terms and conditions set out in your "contract"
- Any other legally binding agreements that have been made before your contract was signed or after, and any changes to such[17]
- All relevant legislation and binding law (such as the Employment Rights Act 1996)
- Implied terms - these are things that courts will assume everyone meant even if they aren't written, such as the right not to have anyone hit you at work as a valid form of management intervention.

ASIDE - OK so I'm not an employment lawyer, although I do have a law degree and have spent 25 years dealing with the implications of employment law. I do explain my understanding of a few things in this book because otherwise the story wouldn't necessarily make sense, but PLEASE PLEASE PLEASE don't use this as some sort of strange employment law primer,

OK so, realising that this small team of six or seven women had always been classified as "casual workers" irrespective of how long they had worked at the council, I needed to see what this meant, and whether it was going to be a problem.

Being a casual worker at ENC meant the following:

- Lower pay (minimum wage, but lower than any other employee at the council)
- No contractual sick pay (permanent staff got six months full sick pay and six months half pay after five year's service)
- No automatic inclusion in the local government pension scheme (this is worth about 25% of salary, and was a very generous final salary pension scheme, albeit it has changed a lot since then and is now a complicated mess, but that is another story...).
- No enhanced maternity pay, and possibly no maternity pay at all

This was now a complicated mess, but first thing was first, I needed to look to see if these really were zero-hours workers. You see just because you say someone is a zero-hour worker it doesn't mean they are. Courts would look at how many hours you worked and how frequently. Although 42 year's service is clearly substantial, I then needed to look at how consistently that work was done. Were there massive gaps of months and years where the employees did not work?

At this point I did the sensible thing and delegated to my amazing team. I asked them to look back and calculate how much the "casuals" had worked each week and month going back through their entire employment. This obviously took some time, but they did a great piece of work and then gave it back to me with a worried look on their face.

This team of women were not casual workers. They had worked every week and every month, in pretty consistent patterns. Yes, they had taken some breaks, but usually for sickness, holiday and maternity.

They had been underpaid for their entire careers.

They were all women.

I knew that this wasn't going to be popular news to their manager. Their manager was the guy from the bullying story that had told someone that "the shit was going to hit the fan". Not someone I was particularly impressed with. I explained the situation. His response was that he didn't care. He had got away with paying them as casuals for all this time, and he didn't see why he should stop now (he hadn't been in post 42 years, but he had been in post for more than 20 years).

I went to his boss, who came down to my office and told me I'd better stop causing problems.

I went to his boss, who tried to avoid me.

I went to the lawyers and explained the situation.

They realised that this could be a legal, financial and reputational disaster.

Reluctantly David allowed me to write a paper to the Personnel Committee of the Council. I didn't blame anyone, I didn't write a dramatic report, I just explained the situation and the risks and asked for two things.

1. That this team be paid fairly at Grade 1 with immediate effect, and that they get the same sick pay, annual leave and pension entitlements as everyone else.
2. That they get paid compensation for years of unpaid sick pay, annual leave, pensions and maternity leave.

On the morning of the committee meeting, I walked into the Chamber of the Council. There were seven other papers on the meeting that day, the Chief Executive David Oliver, and a number of senior officers and Directors were due to be there to present their own papers (including the Head of Service responsible for Revs and Bens).

The leader of the council was there, and the deputy leader, and the chair of the committee and three other Elected Councillors.

No other officer showed up. It was just me.

It was just me and the Councillors and the minute taker.

The Leader of the Council was furious and started ringing to try and get the other officers to come into the room.

None could be found.

The meeting went ahead with me as the only officer.

I had to present my paper, and all of the others (some of which I hadn't seen until that meeting).

They agreed to pay the whole team at grade 1 with immediate effect.

They refused to pay any backpay.

From recollection I think their words were "They can sue us if they like, but we aren't paying them a penny in backpay unless we have to, it will cost us a bloody fortune".

I left the room shaking.

The full force of all their anger had been directed at me.

It wasn't really my fault.

But I was the only officer in the room.

I went and hid in my car and cried my eyes out.

Then I dried my eyes and went back to my office and got on with my job.

Nobody ever spoke to me about what had happened ever again. But I put through all the payroll changes myself.

Well actually one person did come and speak to me.

After the next payroll, a rather timid member of the "casual" team knocked on my office door.

She came straight up to me and gave me a bear hug, and started crying.

She just said "thank you".

It was all very uncomfortable. I'm not very good at people being nice to me and thanking me. I find it much easier to cope with people shouting at me.

I probably shouldn't have asked the next question, but I had to say something to break the silence.

"So why did you not say something before?"

I asked - subtle Aime!

"Because we were scared, we thought if we said anything we would lose our jobs, and not be able to feed our children or pay the bills..."

Fuck, fuck, fuck...

Me, well I just felt guilty then that I hadn't got them the backpay...

But sitting here typing this now, with tears in my eyes, I'm realising again. Well, I did my best, and it wasn't easy, I did my best, it wasn't good enough, but I did my best. And well, I guess I did what no-one else was prepared to do.

I simply did the right thing.

But that itch hadn't exactly gone away. It had just moved. If something like this had been allowed to happen, what else was going on? I followed my itch a bit more, but before I tell you the next bit of the story, I need to explain a bit more about how local government pay is actually supposed to work.

Equal pay is a messy issue. The idea is simple, everyone should get paid the same for the same work, irrespective of gender, race, age or any other protected characteristic. Easy right?

But in practice it is really difficult.

How do you tell when two jobs are exactly the same? How can you measure different jobs against each other? How can you deal with market forces and personal performance variation?

East Northamptonshire Council had adopted the National Joint Council (NJC) Job Evaluation Scheme. This was a scheme agreed across multiple local authorities and Trade Unions that is detailed, complicated and took years to agree and implement. The scheme evaluates thirteen factors required by jobs across the council:

1. Knowledge - this includes qualifications and gets more points than the other factors
2. Mental Skills - how much analysis and interpretation does the role require?
3. Interpersonal Communication Skills - written and verbal
4. Physical skills - this might include the skills required to be a plumber, electrician or forklift truck driver
5. Initiative and independence - how much does the person in this role have to get on with without someone in their field to report to? How much responsibility do they have?
6. Physical Demands - a low score in most local authority jobs, but a gardener for example would score high.
7. Mental demands - this is about length of time, does this person have to go to long meetings without breaks, or do long complicated work without the opportunity to change task?
8. Emotional Demands - does the role require the holder to deal with demanding situations, and customers (think social workers and people that deal with angry customers)
9. Responsibility for people - what impact on society does the role have? A town planner for example would score highly here
10. Responsibility for supervision - how many people does this person manage? The more people the higher the score.
11. Responsibility for financial resources - how much money does this role manage and how much sign off do they have personally?

12. Responsibility for physical resources - the highest scores here tend to go to people who have to maintain large databases and highly secure data but they also go to roles where people are estates managers.
13. Working conditions - rare for this to be high in offices, but if someone is working say at a hazardous waste site, they would get higher points here.

I have been responsible for managing and implementing various job evaluation schemes at various employers, including the NHS scheme (joy of joys).

At ENC I was responsible for running the Job Evaluation Scheme using a team of trained evaluators. I arranged the training for the evaluators, dealt with queries and all the appeals, and advised the managers on completing the paperwork (the questionnaire is 56 pages long).

Once a job has been evaluated against the thirteen factors above, each role is given a score (by adding up the points). Groups of points are then split into grades. ENC had 10 grades (1 to 10). Everyone except the Chief Executive and one Director had a role that was graded using this scheme.

Within each grade, there are then 5 spinal column points. This basically means that if you are put on grade 5 at the bottom of the grade, each year you will move up one of the spinal column points until you get to the top of the grade (this is automatic and not dependent on performance, but that is another story entirely).

After the issue with the casual staff, I started looking at the grading scheme and how it had been implemented before I started. This was about the time that organisations had to start publishing equal pay data. David Oliver was certain that the scheme under his watch had been run amazingly. He asked me to do an equal pay audit, expecting it to show how amazing ENC and he had been.

When I analysed all the figures for ENC during the equal pay audit[18] I compared where men and women started on their grade.

Did they all start at the bottom?

No they didn't and there was a stark gender difference.

92% of women started on the bottom SCP (as the policy stated they should).

But only 44% of men started at the bottom.

Or put another way:

56% of men were bumped up the scale when they started.

Compared with only 8% of women.

So how did that happen you might ask?

Well, the policy states that everyone starts at the bottom. But in exceptional circumstances, the Chief Executive, and the Chief Executive alone, has the power to offer more money. And David Oliver had been doing it a lot, for men, but not so much for women.

Fuck, how the hell was I going to raise this with David? He thinks the sun shines out of his arse and thinks he's like the best, most kindest, most generous and fair boss in the universe, how the hell was I going to tell him that the figures show he was being sexist?

David is an accountant by background, so I decided to simply report all the figures. No drama, no accusations. I just wrote the report, and put all the figures in. I then wrote a paragraph about the need to look further into why this variation might have happened, and how it could be amended.

I sent it off to him in draft.

He called me into his office and lost his shit.

Apparently, he didn't like the inference that anything had been done wrong, and he wanted me to change the report to say so.

I refused.

Initially...

But then figured it wasn't a fight worth fighting and reworded the paragraph as David had told me to:

5.5 As this is the first year that this assessment has been undertaken, there are no facts, or on-going trends to suggest this represents a problem. However, the process of agreeing starting salaries and training for recruiting managers will be provided and increased monitoring will take place.

Yep, that will do it, let's blame the managers, because after all it's always their fault.

None of this sat well with me, but I hoped that now that it had been brought to his attention, it would stop.

It didn't.

And no-one ever did an equal pay audit ever again.

I tried to get the process changed, and formalised, so that we could ensure that women were being treated equally, but David just blocked me at every turn.

So, feeling I had no choice, I decided to do the one thing no employer ever wants their HR Manager to do. I put in my own equal pay claim (remember those emails?).

I put in my equal pay claim in February 2018 with two grounds:

1. Women, including myself were being put on the bottom of the grade when they started.
2. A particular man, let's call him Dave, was appointed on a grade higher than me without his role being job evaluated, even though his job was similar to mine.

It was no easier to get ENC to consider my equal pay than it was to get them to look at my whistleblowing allegations or the bullying issues, but well, I'm quite determined, so again I went to external audit, and they forced an investigation to be done.

In July 2020, more than two years after I'd put in my original claim, a report finally turned up.

Things had got a little better, and they did analyse the data between 2010 and 2018 and found that:[19]

76% of women had been appointed at the bottom of the grade.

And 59% of men had been appointed at the bottom of the grade.

Better, but still not great. Put another way:

41% of men were given higher than basic starting salaries and

24% of women were given higher than basic starting salaries

It should be exactly the same, especially over such a long frame of reference (which should even out any minor statistical anomalies).

The investigation looked for the reasons why the decisions were made by David to appoint above the bottom of the salary, and only found reasons for 63% of the decisions. No record was made for the others, David just decided.

But of course, without the reasons (and the report never shared those - I doubt there was much written down even for those where there was said to be a reason) it is impossible to tell whether the decisions made were fair. Maybe more women than men should have been offered higher salaries... we will never know.

When Interviewed by the investigator and asked his reasons for appointing at higher salaries he said "...a combination of factors such as the candidate's current salary level, significant experience, knowledge or skills required for the role, and/or labour market challenges in recruiting into certain roles".

I had been Head of HR Shared Services and Head of Learning and Development in the NHS across seven Trusts earning £56,000 before I had been made redundant when the PCT's were merged into super PCTs. I had needed a job locally where I could still drop off and pick up the girls from nursery (as my ex-husband was a paramedic and did shift work). I have undergraduate degrees in law, psychology and a masters in HR. The new job was almost £20,000 lower than my previous role (at the bottom of the scale), but I was told that everyone was appointed at the bottom of the scale, and I accepted that.

You can see why I was a tad annoyed... it took me five years to get to the top of the scale and the difference in salary over that time was more than £10,000...

The problem with David Oliver making these decisions, not recording them and then after the fact attempting to justify them, is that there wasn't transparency with the decision making. The decisions are subjective and open not only to potentially direct sexism but also unconscious bias. We all have unconscious biases, they are buried in our decision-making systems, and we don't even know that we are using them. For example most people tend to assume a doctor will be a man and a nurse will be a woman, without actually believing that all doctors are men or even that women shouldn't be doctors - it is just an inbuilt assumption about what is likely.

So how should David and ENC have handled this better? Well back in 2013, when I did the first equal pay audit, instead of getting defensive and shouting at me, David could have sat down and thought about it, and put in place a mechanism to record his reasons for making decisions and to try to eliminate any subconscious bias. And then we could have worked together to ensure that whatever exceptions he was making, they didn't unduly benefit men. And this wouldn't have turned into such a long drawn-out and painful process where nobody really won.

But that requires real leadership, and the capacity to see beyond one's own ego and do the right thing...

But when the councillors read the report they decided that it was all OK. All David's decisions had been OK, and nothing needed to change. The Councillor who chaired the final decision was Helen Harrison, who is currently the Conservative candidate in the Wellingborough by-election.

How are we ever going to get equal pay, if things like this happen in our public organisations?

But I had put in two equal pay claims. The other issue was more blatant...

Dave was appointed while I was on holiday, and was never job evaluated. David Oliver decided to pay him a Grade 10 salary without going through the job evaluation process.

All through the investigation David tried to argue that Dave's post had been job evaluated, but that the paperwork had merely been lost.

Under oath in court it was admitted that there had never been a job evaluation for Dave's post, David had just decided to award him grade 10 on a whim (I was a grade 9).

But not having a job evaluation done, whilst poor, wasn't proof that Dave had been paid more than me unfairly. The role needed to be evaluated to see what grade it would come out as.

ENC appointed an external expert in Local Government Job Evaluation Schemes. He evaluated Dave's role and sent me and the council a copy of the evaluation scores.

He graded Dave as a Grade 9. The same grade as me. Slam dunk, you might have thought, but the situation did not end there. By this point I had already left ENC and put in an employment tribunal claim for a breach of Equal Pay Legislation. This result was a disaster for their defence.

But before it got to the employment tribunal, the report went to, yes you guessed it, a panel of Elected Councillors.

And they decided that everyone had been paid fairly, and no one had done anything wrong.

And then the lawyers spoke to the investigator and asked him to change his analysis, and increase the score from a Grade 9 to a Grade 10. Which he did. Because they asked him to and told him why he should do it. And because well they were paying him.

And this is why we still don't have equal pay for women in the UK despite the fact that the Equal Pay Act came out more than 50 years ago.

It isn't because people are sitting down and deciding to pay women less. It is because the systems and people's attitudes are weighted towards paying men more. Senior management is awash with unconscious bias. And if the figures look a bit dodgy, or someone raises a concern, instead of trying to solve the problem, they try to hide that there is even a problem in the first place...

PART TWO:
The Backlash

Chapter 6
So what is a good girl?

So, I have set the scene. You have seen the issues that I had with ENC and David Oliver, but what happened next?

In the next chapters I am going to tell you how David and his chums reacted to my rather assertive claims that things were not OK. But before I do that, I want to talk a bit about the notion of a "good girl" and the far more healthy "free woman". This story is about my journey from being a people pleaser who blamed myself when things went wrong, even when I shouldn't have, to a woman who accepts her flaws and her mistakes and is accountable for them, but doesn't beat herself up. And it was standing up for myself, and others, that helped free me.

I don't know what you think about the terms good girl and free woman, but after lots of thought, and soul searching, this is where I've got to in my thinking...

Humans are social creatures. In evolutionary terms, when we lived in small hunter gatherer groups, being part of your tribe would have literally been a matter of life or death.

Evolution works slowly, after more than seven million years of hominid evolution, Homo sapiens are the only surviving branch of the hominin family tree[20]. Albeit some of us have a little homo neanderthalensis in us too (including me according to the DNA profile I had done). Our nearest non hominid relatives are chimpanzees and bonobos. A bonobo's DNA is closer to a human's than it is to a Gorilla's.

Homo sapiens or humans appeared in Africa about 200,000 years ago.

It isn't clear how many humans survived the ice age, but it may have been as low as about 180,000. For most of our history before the ice age we were foragers, but evidence of farming can be found in different locations across the globe from about 23,000 years ago as the planet started to warm. Perhaps the near starvation of the survivors of the ice age led to a desire to ensure that food was never sparse again. Farming entered Europe around 7,000 BCE and was the main way of life across Europe by 4,000 BCE.

Farming created the opportunity for a different social structure. With some people being freed from the need to find food, they learnt different skills and became weavers, blacksmiths and the first lawyers and doctors. These changes then led to the creation of towns and cities. Colchester in Essex was the first place in Britain to be given the status of a Roman Town in AD49, and is arguably the first city in the UK. The Roman Fort of Londinium (the beginning of today's London) was built north-west of the main population settlement around AD 110 - 120.

By 1100 AD the population of England was about two million, still relatively small by today's standards. By 1685 it was five million. It hit nine million in 1805. Today the population of the UK is a little over 67 million.

You may be wondering at this point. Well why the abbreviated history of human's Aime?

My point is this.

Although we now have computers and airplanes, dishwashers and iPhones, in evolutionary terms we are still the same humans that survived the ice age. We survived as a species because we were social. We used our larger brains to work together to create tools and learn. But we didn't evolve to live in cities, we evolved to live in small groups no bigger than 150. Farming, and indeed the industrial revolution have led to many amazing advances, but the growth of population sizes isn't something that we evolved to deal with.

Dunbar's number[21] suggests that humans (including us modern ones) can only maintain 150 relationships. And that number is pretty stable through different cultures, and throughout our history. The evolutionary social brain hypothesis[22] suggests that we needed larger brains to maintain so many relationships. Dunbar's number can also be broken down into

Inner Circle .... 5 people

Good Friends .... 15 people

Friends.......... .... 50 people

Meaningful contacts .... 80 people (plus the above)

Beyond this the suggestion is that we might have up to 500 acquaintances and 1,500 people we can recognise (which includes famous people!). Although there is a suggestion that very sociable and extroverted people have larger numbers in their inner circles and friendship groups, even the most social of us still tend to maintain an overall group of no more than 150 meaningful contacts.

The long and short of it is that we are still homo sapiens that evolved to live in social groups. Being ostracised from the group, often meant actual death. If you were banished from your social group a thousand years ago, you were unlikely to be accepted by another group, and unlikely to survive, because surviving on your own was nearly impossible. If you hurt yourself and were not able to get water for three days, with no-one to help, and no fridge or taps, you would have died.

Today, we all have the potential to be connected to many more people than our hunter gatherer ancestors, and it is very possible to move across numerous groups both physically and increasingly digitally. Being banished by one social group is no longer likely to lead to death, but it still feels like it might. The social rules in 2023 may be very different than they were in 10,000 BCE, but the fear of being ostracised is just as bad. In fact, it hurts.[23]

The Good Girl is a cultural script that women are expected to follow to be accepted by themselves, other women, men and society. Or in other words, if you want to be accepted, and survive, then you need to be accepted socially. And to be accepted socially in the modern western world, many of us have been conditioned to believe that we must be a "Good Girl". Although I didn't think of it in these terms then, I too had accepted a model of what I "should be" that was along the lines of the "Good Girl".

Dr. Susan Albers[24] suggests that the need to be a good girl can have a negative impact on women's mental health, and the ability to be happy in day-to-day life and relationships. She describes the six traits of what she terms "Good Girl Syndrome" as

1. Perfectionism
2. People-pleasing
3. Putting other people first
4. Issues with Body Image
1. Sexual difficulties (good girls are meant to be innocent and pure, not have their own sexual needs and desires - this can create distress and guilt about women exploring or enjoying their own sexuality)
2. Hypervigilance - sometimes women's desire to people please and be perfect are a response to earlier trauma. The nervous system attempting to be on the lookout at all times for harm, and then trying to avoid it. We all know about fight or flight as a stress response, but freeze and faun are even more common, especially in women.

Gloria's speech in the recent Barbie film seems to have caught the essence of how women feel that the idea of being a woman is simply impossible to maintain, the ultimate double bind.

> ***"It is literally impossible to be a woman. You are so beautiful, and so smart, and it kills me that you don't think you're good enough. Like, we have to always be extraordinary, but somehow, we're always doing it wrong.***
>
> ***You have to be thin, but not too thin. And you can never***

say you want to be thin. You have to say you want to be healthy, but also you have to be thin. You have to have money, but you can't ask for money because that's crass. You have to be a boss, but you can't be mean. You have to lead, but you can't squash other people's ideas. You're supposed to love being a mother, but don't talk about your kids all the damn time. You have to be a career woman but also always be looking out for other people.

You have to answer for men's bad behavior, which is insane, but if you point that out, you're accused of complaining. You're supposed to stay pretty for men, but not so pretty that you tempt them too much or that you threaten other women because you're supposed to be a part of the sisterhood.

But always stand out and always be grateful. But never forget that the system is rigged. So, find a way to acknowledge that but also always be grateful.

You have to never get old, never be rude, never show off, never be selfish, never fall down, never fail, never show fear, never get out of line. It's too hard! It's too contradictory and nobody gives you a medal or says thank you! And it turns out in fact that not only are you doing everything wrong, but also everything is your fault.

I'm just so tired of watching myself and every single other woman tie herself into knots so that people will like us. And if all of that is also true for a doll just representing women, then I don't even know."

I think this speech resonated with a lot of women because it explains the impossibility of the standards that we are holding ourselves and other women to.

It is impossible to actually "be" a good girl. But that is the ideal we inspire to anyway.

Our evolution has left us with brains and nervous systems that are programmed to seek social acceptance in order to survive.

And not being good enough might lead to rejection and social ostracisation, which our nervous systems process as both physically painful, and potentially life threatening. So, we desperately try to meet this impossible "Good Girl" ideal and mostly spend our lives feeling we have failed or are not good enough.

But it is an impossible ideal.

So.

If it's impossible.

And it's all a load of socially constructed bollocks, that keeps women feeling shit.

Then there is only one solution.

To hack our own social conditioning.

And become free women.

And this is my story of how I tried, and I think succeeded.

Although it was bloody painful, nearly killed me, and I'm not sure I'm totally out the other side yet...

(And side note, there is a whole lot of unhelpful social conditioning about masculinity too, and I think men should hack the hell out of that too and find out what it is to be a free man, but that isn't my story, so I haven't talked about that in this book).

Chapter 7
Three old men or three little boys?

Before I tell you happened next, I need to tell you a bit about the men who were involved.

There were three men at ENC that had a problem with me. One was David Oliver, the Chief Executive, you've already heard quite a bit about him.

The second was Glenn Hammons, the new Chief Financial Officer, who became my line manager. I'm going to tell you a bit about him in this chapter.

Both David and Glenn upset me, but they didn't scare me.

The third man stills scares me.

I've thought long and hard about whether I should include his name here, but I've decided against it.

Whilst I am trying to do the right thing and be honest and upfront with the aim of trying to get organisations to treat staff better, I still have a right to keep myself safe. So, I reserve the right to withhold the name of the third man for the sake of my own on-going wellbeing.

You have already heard a bit about how David Oliver treated me at the end but let me tell you a bit more about what happened before that.

David Oliver didn't appoint me, but in my role running the HR for the council, I had dealings with him as the Chief Executive frequently, and for about a year and a half he was my direct line manager.

Have you read the book *"The Authority Gap"* by Mary Ann Sieghart? She suggests that women have to work so much harder to be given the same authority as men, and that often women aren't accepted as authorities even if they very much deserve it.

My approach to this problem was to try to prove that I was worthy of being given that authority. I'm not sure if that was the right approach, and in hindsight it probably backfired (the better I was at my job the more threatening I seemed).

When I got the job as HR Manager at East Northamptonshire Council I was already a qualified and very experienced HR professional.

But still I wasn't treated with much respect by David. Because obviously as an accountant he knew far more than me about everything. Once, he criticised the financial tests I had set for the Head of Finance as being too hard... in hindsight doing the test myself and getting a better mark than all the applicants was probably not such a great idea, but I was just trying to show that it wasn't that hard... you know like if the HR Manager can do it, then it can't be that difficult... I hadn't realised at the time I had also beaten the score he got... and the gossip was that he had got a third at University and was a little sore about it. So, talking about being accepted onto the Phd programme and getting the HR lecturing request probably wasn't a great idea. But hindsight is a wonderful thing...

David loved to tell me I didn't know what I was talking about. At one point he commissioned an external company to sort out the IT department (some of our systems and equipment were ancient) and we'd lost two IT Directors in three years. I offered to help with the HR aspect of the project, looking at job redesigns, and redeployment etc. He told me that I wasn't needed as he "had real experts" doing the role, and that as consultants he was paying them a lot as they were worth it. The truth was that they hadn't got much experience of local government, so whilst they did know a lot about IT, they didn't understand job evaluation, or our policies and procedures.

They met with me and asked me to write out a draft plan that included all the HR implications of the project. My basic approach is generally that it is more important to get the job done, rather than take credit for the work. I wanted the project to work, and I didn't want the staff to be unduly messed about with messy processes, so I wrote out a ten page plan and sent it to them.

In my next one to one with David, he said that he needed to talk me through the HR plan for the IT change project and gave me a copy of my own plan, with the consultancy's logo at the top.

They hadn't changed a word.

I had a quick look and explained to David that I had written the document. He told me not to be "silly". He suggested that whilst I may have helped them a little, they were the experts and had taken a few of my ideas and incorporated them into this excellent plan.

He then spent an hour mansplaining my own document to me.

I don't think he ever believed that I had written it.

I will do difficult things. I will do painful things. If it needs doing, then I will do it, sometimes at great cost to myself, but nonetheless I would do it. I'm not sure this is bravery, it is just the way I'm made, it is probably just insanity, it really doesn't feel like a choice.

There are several times when David struggled to do something and tried to get me to do it for him instead.

He didn't like it if anyone embarrassed him. There was once an amazing manager, who did a really good job, a little too well, and she did something that made him look a bit silly. Instead of dealing with it, he blamed her. She hadn't been there very long so he decided we should sack her on the spot without any process. I tried to reason with him, I tried to argue with him. But he told me that it was his choice and if I didn't do it he would sack me instead.

I walked to her office and tried to explain to her the best I could what had happened.

It felt wrong. Maybe I should have walked out that day, or refused, but I hadn't been there that long, and I believed that he would sack me if I didn't do it.

I went with another manager, and we did it together.

The individual was shocked. What no process? No appeal? No opportunity to state her case?

No, we said, and she needed to leave her office right now and never come back. We escorted her to her car.

It was horrible.

She was understandably upset. I rang her every day for a week to check she was OK. I was worried she might do something to hurt herself, sometimes people do in these circumstances. I only stopped ringing her when she had said she was going to see her GP and had family coming to stay and was going to see a counsellor. I stopped calling her when I knew that she would be OK.

And I got in trouble for calling her. Apparently, I was overstepping my role, putting the council at risk, meddling.

It wasn't my job to check she was OK apparently, just to sack her.

It wasn't the last time David struggled to sack someone himself. There was another person who was struggling with their health. They were an amazing manager, but had been off sick for a long time, and the doctor's reports said they were unlikely to ever return. Part of the reason they were sick was the toxic environment they were working in, including reporting to David Oliver. I sat together with David and did the final hearing.

We asked the employee to leave for a bit while we discussed what to do next, but there was really no option other than to end their employment. They had run out of sick pay; we had tried everything. David asked if I could go and tell the person the outcome. I said no, I didn't have the authority to dismiss this person on my own, he needed to do it.

He instantly looked embarrassed, we both knew he had asked me to do something he didn't want to do. I went and got the individual and he came back in.

After fifteen minutes of small talk, I realised David wasn't going to be able to say the words, so I said them as supportively and kindly as I could.

I got a thank you email from the employee later.

They said that whilst they didn't want to go, and wished there could have been another way, they understood the decision. They thanked me for supporting them and treating them with dignity and kindness throughout the process.

I'm still proud of that email, I did good, but in hindsight did I do too well? I don't think David liked how it went.

I spoke to a number of people about how to deal with David's behaviour, and they all told me it was my job to try and handle him. That although he was my boss, it was my responsibility to make sure that I didn't upset and irritate him. That I should try to appease him, and learn how to behave in a way that he liked, and that way he wouldn't get angry at me, or shout at me. I tried, but he still shouted at me.

I don't cry easily or often, but he made me cry numerous times. Usually, I managed to get away from him and back to my office before I burst into tears, so at least I could cry in private.

I thought about leaving, but I'd begun to believe what he said, I thought maybe I wasn't very good at my job, maybe I wasn't cut out to be a senior manager. I needed my job to pay the bills, I just didn't have it in me to start anywhere new.

David didn't like me leaving meetings without his permission. This made me feel totally trapped. No matter how I felt, or if I had another meeting, or had to pick up the kids, I wasn't allowed to leave. I'm a middle-aged professional, obviously I'm not just going to abandon a meeting for no reason, but where did I sign to say I wasn't allowed to leave without permission. Surely that isn't OK in employment? I tried to excuse myself assertively but politely, and most of the time it worked, but sometimes it didn't, and he got angry.

The meetings I hated most were the Trade Union meetings. Me, David, and the two senior Trade Union officers would be present, we would get lots of useful things discussed, but they often descended into chats. It was OK when both Trade Union officers were present, but not when it was just David and one of the Trade Union officers. Strangely they were good friends, and neither liked me very much, so they would sometimes try to bait me, or just spend half an hour telling me all the things they didn't like about me and what I was doing wrong.

They thought it was funny to "bait" the HR Manager with things that were decidedly un-PC. They once spent 20 minutes discussing a TV programme that they had both watched about a man's enlarged testicle. To be honest, other than being a complete waste of my time and in bad taste, I wasn't too bothered about that, I just started planning some work I needed to do.

But another day the conversation got far more unpleasant. They were talking about the police and they were talking about police hats. They began to wonder what trans police officers would wear (although their terminology was less pleasant). Then David said something that truly upset me.

"Well, I think it is ridiculous, you are whatever gender you are born, I don't believe in all of this ridiculousness about changing genders. People should just accept that they are the gender based on what is between their legs".

I was shocked, not just that he should think it, but that he should think it was OK to share such transphobic opinions as the Chief Executive of a public body.

After the meeting I explained that I was upset about what he said. He seemed surprised and said something like "but you aren't one of them are you Aime?".

I said that whilst I wasn't, I had friends that were, and that anyway, I was insulted, and that I didn't expect to hear that kind of attitude at work, let alone from the mouth of the Chief Executive. He glared at me and told me it was probably time I went home and made my husband dinner.

Writing all of these down does feel a little bizarre. Why did I ever think any of this was my fault? But when you are in it, it feels wrong, but it just didn't feel clear what I could do about it.

So now you've got an idea of the kind of person David Oliver was. Now I need to introduce you to the other protagonist, Glenn Hammons.

Glenn Hammons made quite an impression the first time I met him. Quiet but confident, he looked significantly more dapper than the majority of Local Government Officers in his three-piece suits. However, it slowly emerged that whilst he might look the part, and he could certainly talk a good talk, there was not much substance below the facade.

Before Glenn Hammons came to work at ENC, he had spent his entire working career at Northamptonshire County Council starting with them as an apprentice.

Northamptonshire County Council talked a big talk, and in meetings had a tendency to act as the more important partner when they met with little old East Northamptonshire Council. But behind the scenes, after years of poor strategy and financial decision making, as well as pressures from reduced government income and increased demands on their services, they were slowly going bankrupt.

Glenn had spent the majority of his career at NCC slowly working his way up in the Finance Department. Whilst Glenn was Head of Finance and Business Intelligence for NCC the decision was made to freeze council tax. A Conservative led council, they kept the council tax lower than most councils across the country, cutting services and resources to their departments instead.

But they didn't have enough money to pay their bills, even with the cuts, so NCC started keeping itself afloat by selling its assets.

Whilst popular with voters initially, this financial strategy led to NCC being the first Council to go bankrupt in 20 years (although many have followed suit, including Birmingham and Nottingham in recent months). They also failed to deliver key services. Ofsted reported that Children's Social Care Services were "failing to keep children safe" and that there were "highly vulnerable children in care who were living in unregulated placements that are unsafe and unsuitable".[25]

Glenn continued to be employed by NCC as a senior Finance official until February 2018, just as NCC went officially bankrupt. Central Government stepped in appointing new leadership. Following an independent investigation[26] into financial and governance failings at the council, deemed to be beyond fixing, Northamptonshire County Council was scrapped in April 2021, it's services distributed between two new authorities.[27] Although they are still arguing about the finances more than two years after the creation of the new councils.[28]

Between early 2013 and February 2018, in an attempt to bring in some extra funds to the cash strapped NCC, Glenn Hammons was seconded part-time to be the Chief Finance Officer (and Section 151 Officer) at Northampton Borough Council alongside his other duties.

In 2013 Northampton Town Football Club (NTFC) were in the second division. While Glenn was overseeing the finances of Northampton Borough Council, the Council made a decision to loan around £10 million to NTFC to expand the East and West Stands and create a range of new facilities, including a conference centre, a 100 room hotel, a gym and up to 300 new homes and offices.

The Cabinet delegated authority to the Chief Executive (David Kennedy) and Glenn Hammons to make the loans, subject to ensuring that a number of conditions were met. These conditions included the requirement to ensure that there was sufficient security offered for the loan, and that there were robust contractual arrangements in place. But there was no security for the loan and robust contractual arrangements were not put in place.

Northampton Borough Council borrowed the money and loaned it to Northampton Town Football Club.

Works started and initially the loan repayments were met, but within a few months works ground to a halt, as did the repayments.

The works were never finished, and the money seemingly vanished, all £10 million of it.

Northampton Borough Council were left with a £10 million loan, no collateral, no repayments, and no redeveloped football club, just a very large bill, and egg on their faces.

It was such a disaster the police got involved.

The police began Operation Tuckhill to try and find out where the money had gone, and whose fault it was it had gone missing. Operation Tuckhill is a complex financial and corruption investigation that has led to allegations of theft, fraud, money laundering, bribery and misconduct in public office and is still ongoing. I've provided a link to the BBC summary of the events that led up to the disappearing money here[29] and a link to the BBC summary of the police investigation here.[30]

Glenn Hammons was responsible for advising the council on this loan, and has been heavily criticised for his involvement, and interviewed under caution for potential criminal offences related to his involvement in the missing money by the police four times.

All councils have both internal and external auditors who check through the accounts. They are appointed to ensure that there is no wrongdoing, and that the spending of our hard earned money is done with due diligence and within the law.

In early 2021 KPMG, Northampton Borough Council's external auditor made the incredibly rare decision to publish a Public Interest Report into the disappearance of the £10 million loan.

The report concluded that the "serious failings" in the council's "arrangements" over the loan and the financial exposure without appropriate risk mitigation "rendered the decisions unlawful".[31]

The report was critical of Glenn Hammon's involvement stating that he "fell short, in KPMG's view, of his duty to the protect the financial interests of the council - and its taxpayers and residents".

In July 2018 Northampton Borough Council took legal action in an attempt to recoup some of the lost funds.[32] In cross examination Glenn Hammons admitted that

a) he had received complimentary Spurs tickets as gifts from the businessman Howard Grossman, but had failed to declare them.

b) that he had been interviewed under caution four times in relation to Operation Tuckhill.

c) that he had attended numerous working lunches and dinners provided by Howard Grossman, but had failed to declare them.

Howard Grossman was 1st Land's Ltd sole director. 1st Land Ltd was the development company that received the money that went missing. He has since been banned from being a company director and been made bankrupt. I believe his wife is currently having their house repossessed in order to repay some of the money that went missing.[33]

All public sector organisations such as councils have strict rules about not receiving gifts, and any gifts submitted over £5 have to be registered and handed over. They are often raffled for charity. Glenn's excuse about not registering the gifts was that he didn't know who to tell.

It is my opinion that he should have known not to accept the gifts in the first place, but if he did decide to accept them they should have been reported and logged. These policies are in place to ensure not only that there is no corruption, but that there can't even be seen to be any suggestion of corruption.

There is perhaps an assumption that the tickets were just the normal £60 tickets. However a BBC article revealed that 1st Land Ltd had spent £36,000 on Spurs Tickets.[34] It is not clear what level of Spurs tickets were given to Glenn, but it is entirely possible that he received one of the far more expensive hospitality tickets, which can cost more than £10,000. If this is the case, then it would be far worse, but even a single Spurs ticket is, in my opinion, inappropriate. I once gave in a tray of Dunkin Donuts from a recruitment agency because they were above the £5 allowed! (And I like doughnuts!).

We've all watched plenty of police dramas and we know the difference between being arrested and being a witness. An interview under caution is often used by the police where they believe a crime may have been committed, but do not wish to make an arrest (or do not have enough evidence to make an arrest). Interviews under caution are not done lightly, and witnesses are not interviewed in this way. To be interviewed under caution means that the police thought that Glenn might have committed a crime.

Operation Tuckhill is still ongoing, so we aren't sure at this point whether the police may have dropped all investigations into Glenn, or whether they may still arrest him at some point. What we do know is that they had enough evidence/concern to interview him under caution four times. (If you'd like to read a bit more, here is Newcastle City Council's guidance on interviewing under caution).[35]

Because it had been reported extensively in the press, I was aware that Glenn was being investigated by the police for his role in the missing £10 million loan when David Oliver informed me that he had slotted Glenn into the role of Executive Director at East Northamptonshire Council without an advert or interviews.

I was concerned that the correct recruitment processes had not been followed. As the Executive Director role included the duty of being a s151 officer (a technical role whose appointment rules are set out in the Local Government Act 1972), I knew that this required several processes to be followed to appoint to the role. The role was legally required to be advertised and appropriate recruitment checks (including police record checks) were standard.

I spoke to the Monitoring Officer (the person at the council responsible for legal compliance) and was told that David Oliver had advised the elected officials that no checks were needed in the case of Glenn. I was told to not get references, to not check Glenn had the correct references, and was told it was OK in these circumstances to simply slot Glenn in without advertising the role or holding any interviews.

As you can imagine, I was not happy with this. On a professional level, I would have objected to it under normal circumstances, but with Glenn currently under police investigation this seemed to be very odd indeed. I was told I should just do as I was told, and that Glenn would be my line manager and would deal with me personally. Great... just great... this is going to be so much fun...

So, without a competitive process, or any interviews or appropriate checks, a man who was being investigated by the police was appointed as my boss and put in charge of East Northamptonshire Council's Finances just as his old Council filed for bankruptcy. An excellent recruitment choice in my humble opinion...

My guess is that Glenn needed a lifeboat before he got into incredibly choppy water at both Northamptonshire County Council and Northampton Borough Council, and his good friend

David Oliver was happy to provide him with a nice safe job with a hefty salary as that lifeboat. Ironic perhaps that a Conservative run council is much happier about providing metaphorical lifeboats to one of its own, but less keen on doing so for refugees running for their life with their children whose lives are at risk for no fault of their own.

The pink paper that advised the council of the decision to appoint Glenn, actually has a paragraph on the equality and diversity implications (paragraph 4.3) and it says

"Slotting in Glenn Hammons could arguably not be advancing equality of opportunity for anyone with a protected characteristic who would be eligible to apply for the role if it were advertised externally. However, to go through an external appointment process would be time-consuming and expensive and would be unlikely to produce a better candidate"

I mean no woman or black person, or even another white male accountant in the whole of the UK could possibly be as skilled as Glenn...

I had challenged the process of Glenn's appointment, and he was not very happy with me doing this. In fact, he was furious.

But I take my job seriously. I was responsible for the HR department, including the recruitment process and recruitment checks and equality and diversity. Dropping someone into a role, with no process, against the rules set out in legislation, and without any adequate reference or police checks, when we all knew that the applicant was being investigated by the police for potential criminal involvement in the missing loan money, just seemed ridiculous.

In the external whistleblowing investigation into the appointment of Glenn Hammons, it is noted[36] that it is legally required by s151 of the Local Government Act 1972 that Chief Finance Appointments should be advertised with a job description and person specification, and this is mirrored in ENC's constitution.

The external investigator interviewed David over Glenn's appointment, and David confirmed that it was a decision made on his recommendation by the Elected councillors. If you are wondering if David Oliver and the councillors knew about the police concerns surrounding Glenn Hammons when they appointed him, then the whistleblowing report confirms that they did.

"DO noted that he was not clear on whether all Council Members were aware of the football club loan but that he would have expected that they were, in view of the publicity the case had attracted and that he is sure that the leader of the council was aware. DO noted that there are not and never have been any concerns in relation to GH's work at ENC"

It appears therefore that Glenn was appointed, without any due process or advert, in full knowledge that he was being investigated by the policy for fraud and the mishandling of the £10 million loan.

The external criticisms of Glenn did not stop after he was given the role at ENC. Other mistakes were also discovered retrospectively about his role at Northampton Borough Council. He was heavily criticised by the external auditors when the cost of signing off the 2016/2017 accounts for Northampton Borough Council hit lengthy delays and the cost of the audit ballooned from £80,000 to around £300,000. Incorrect formula's had been used when valuing properties owned by the council resulting in significantly undervalued estimates of social housing. The audit still had not been completed by August 2018 (i.e. more than a year after the end of the financial year, rare and most would consider unacceptable).

Auditors are not normally noted for their emotive commentary, usually being the careful and quiet types, but the frustrations spilled out into the Northampton Chronicle. Mr Cardozo the auditor was quoted as saying[37]

"This discount factor is normally a tick, but when we asked about it, they gave rubbish answers. They had no idea what a social discount factor was. Our officers found it farcical, there's no other way to put it."

"We have twelve recommendations in detail. Most have already been discussed and all of them have been accepted by officers.

"There are very large numbers that need not have been there if the previous section 151 officer [Glenn Hammons] had checked some of these things. There was also an inadequate handover from the previous section 151 officer [Glenn Hammons] to the current one, so it's not a surprise...the previous section 151 officer [Glenn Hammons] wasn't looking through the stuff that was coming in"

Ouch...

But it doesn't stop there.

Glenn Hammons stayed at East Northamptonshire Council running the finances for some years after I left. In February 2022 police were called to East Northamptonshire Council as it was found that internally someone had set up a direct debit for £100 a week that had been running for 130 weeks without being detected. In total £13,000 was stolen. This fraud was not discovered because no reconciliation of the accounts was ever conducted.[38]

It is hard writing all of this, it just feels so unfair. David Oliver and Glenn Hammons have admitted to doing far worse things than I believe I was ever accused of, yet I was sacked, and they just carried on doing their jobs.

But ultimately I'm trying to be fair to all parties. I am trying to give you the facts, it is you, the reader, the tax payer, who ultimately get to decide whether you are OK with what has happened. Is this how you want your Council's to be run? Are these the kind of people you want to be looking after your money?

Chapter 8
An attempt to tame the shrew

What does an organisation do with a woman like me that has put in three very serious complaints?

The initial responses to my complaints were actually handled quite well. My emails were acknowledged, and I was told they would be looked into. In response to my bullying and harassment claim against the Chief Executive, David Oliver, it was agreed that he would not speak to me, or email me, and on a meeting by meeting basis it would be worked out which of us needed to attend, so I didn't have to see him.

I was hugely relieved.

I'm not sure I realised just how much stress he was causing me, until I suddenly felt safe, knowing that I wouldn't have to deal with his anger and unfairness again.

The time after I put in my complaints was an odd time, in many ways it was the happiest I'd ever been at East Northamptonshire Council, as I could just get on with my job without the bullying, but I was also nervous about what came next, and whilst they seemed to be doing and saying all the right things I still wasn't sure whether they might not just blame me for everything.

I mean that's what happens to women who speak up and tell their truth isn't it?

Suddenly it is the women that are the ones under scrutiny, their legitimacy is questioned, their stories are not believed, until somehow, they go from being the victim to the perpetrator.

I wasn't naive enough to think I would avoid this fate entirely, just hopeful that maybe the world had moved on enough that perhaps any response would at least be balanced and fair, you know, how things should be done, how I would have done them.

This respite was longer than I expected.

Then the pressure started.

It started slowly.

There is a nationally agreed framework for dealing with internal grievances of this nature against a Chief Executive of a Council, and there was a formal procedure for dealing with Whistleblowing complaints. The procedures all require independent investigators and due process.

But of course, that is not what ENC wanted to do.

Glenn Hammons had been appointed as the Chief Financial Officer of the council and had become my line manager around the time I put in my complaints. I was meeting him fairly frequently as he got to grips with his new job and overseeing my area. The pressure started, unexpectedly, in one of those meetings. Although he reported to David Oliver, and was still in his probationary period, Glenn suggested that he had decided that he was going to do all the investigations personally and keep everything in house.

I probably looked at him quizzically. He was going to do the investigation into his boss? I looked at him waiting, I almost thought he was suddenly going to say "just kidding" but no, shit, he was actually being serious.

"It is generally considered inappropriate for anyone to investigate their boss. Especially in their probation period when they are under scrutiny and might fail to secure the job permanently. I'm not sure it would be within the policies for you to do the investigations Glenn" - well I said something like that. In hindsight it may have been a little stronger... I can't quite remember, I was in that strange state where you are thinking "sorry what the fuck is happening here, am I actually still in real life, or did I actually accidentally walk into VR or a dream or something, is this shit for real?"

No, it was very much for real. Over the next few weeks Glenn hassled me over and over again to give him every allegation in writing before the investigations started properly. I slowly realised what was going on. I calmly resisted and stated that once the formal investigation had started and investigating officers appointed in line with the policies, I would submit all of my evidence to them as part of the process.

They waited for months, and no investigating officers were appointed, but then I suddenly got asked to a without prejudice meeting the next day.

Employers and employees are entitled to have "off the books" conversations legally to try to resolve things. I had done a fair few of them before that day, and since I set up the Trade Union and started representing members I've done loads more. In principle they are a good idea, a way for people to try to find a resolution. I could understand that it was not going to be easy to talk about the Chief Executive in an open meeting, so I didn't really feel scared or worried. What happened next however felt completely bizarre, it felt straight out of a Netflix drama film.

I went to the meeting. It had been arranged in the Chief Executive's office. He wasn't there, but that was the first hint I had that it wasn't going to go well. There were plenty of big offices, and Glenn's was more than adequate. They were trying to scare me.

Straight off the bat they got down to business. They basically just wanted to know how much money it was going to take for me to drop all my complaints, leave and sign a non-disclosure agreement (basically agreeing to never tell anyone about anything that had happened). They literally asked me how much money I wanted. Taxpayers money. Your money. They were offering me your hard-earned money, so they didn't have to investigate anything, and their secrets were buried.

"This isn't about money" I said.

Glenn and David are both accountants by trade. They had clearly thought this was just some sort of hustle, I was just after money. Or maybe they just always thought of money as the solution to everything. How much does it cost to make this problem go away? How much taxpayer's money will it cost to get Aime to go away?

They became irritated that I wasn't giving them a figure and that this wasn't going the way they wanted. This was after all just meant to be a financial negotiation. They offered me £30,000 tax free to just leave now. They would give me three months' notice pay as well, and a nice reference.

Well thank you very much.

But no.

This wasn't about the money.

At first, I think they thought I was just a tough negotiator. That I had a much bigger figure in mind and was playing hard ball. In fact, they asked me how much money I would like.

Again, I said that this wasn't about the money.

Slowly the penny dropped.

They realised that maybe it really wasn't about money for me.

And they switched tactics.

"If you don't take the deal, well we have things on you Aime"

What the actual fuck? Had this guy been watching too many gangster films or what? Got something on me? I mean I'm no saint, and I'm sure I've like made a few errors here or there, but I'm not a Mafia boss with a whole load of hidden bodies...

Oh, hold on a second. I remembered that, well people tend to assume everyone is like they are, and map that onto other people. There's a psychological thing, name for it, wasn't it Freud's daughter? Under the stress of the situation my brain was struggling to remember.

They think I'm like them.

They think I'm all about money and that I have loads of dodgy shit I've hidden over the years.

I almost spat my tea out. I'm the good girl, I cried all night when I realised at Brownies that I had underpaid by one pence for my sweets because I had miscounted. There was an honour system, so I'd counted them myself and paid, but when I got home, I counted them again, and realised I'd miscounted, there was one more sweet than I had paid for, therefore I had underpaid. According to my mum I was literally inconsolable and cried for hours, until my parents explained that I could take the one pence the next week, and it would all be OK. Which I did.

So no, I didn't have any big secrets or issues I had hidden. I had always done the job to the best of my abilities, and with the upmost honesty. And generally, I had done my job very well, which is why I had been promoted to be Head of HR Shared Services in the NHS in my twenties... Of course, I will have made mistakes, everyone has, but at that point, I'd passed every audit with flying colours, passed every assessment, every appraisal, and met every KPI. I was doing fairly well at trying to be a "good girl".

To be fair during the meeting. I think I held my cool enough not to actually say "what the fuck".

I wish in hindsight I'd said something really cool like "You ain't got nothing on me", or "Your gonna have to kill me to find out where the bodies are buried". But I can't do cool even when I have plenty of time to think about it. That just isn't who I am. I'm in awe of the amazing scriptwriters who write that cool shit, but it just isn't me. And well, under the pressure of the situation I just asked him what he was talking about.

I shit you not, he then got all like secretive and just said something like "well we've been told you've done stuff". I mean like he probably didn't actually say those words, but something close to that.

Of course, that then sent me into an actual flat panic. I knew I hadn't done anything, but I was suddenly really scared that I had somehow accidentally done something I didn't know about. You know where you start feeling guilty just as a habit, and start blaming yourself you know automatically, even though you can't remember doing anything and the worst I probably did was eat too many doughnuts? But the good girl conditioning just massively kicked in.

At that point it had all got too much. And the meeting clearly wasn't going anywhere, so I suggested that we'd been talking for a long time and it wasn't going anywhere, so maybe we should end the meeting.

It was a beautiful sunny spring afternoon, and I went outside and sat on the bench. It was about five in the afternoon, and I just sat there stunned. Were they actually going to turn this all on me somehow?

The strange thing about living through this, is that it seems so weird at the time, that you just sort of carry on with your normal life as if you are in a haze. Or maybe it was just some sort of shock.

But either way I went in the next day and carried on with my job. I didn't really believe they were going to sack me, or suspend me, because well, that's not really a fair response to me putting in complaints is it?

After working as a Trade Union representative for four years, I now realise that some organisations don't even try to do things fairly, why should they? Yes, there are great employers who do things properly, but most don't. They have all the power, and it is a faff to do it properly. If they can get away with using a bit of taxpayers or shareholders money to save themselves some effort and embarrassment why wouldn't they? I mean they weren't offering me £30,000 of their own money, they were offering me £30,000 or more of your money, to make their lives easier.

At about 9.15 am I got a phone call from Glenn. Odd in itself because his office was only a ninety second walk from mine. He asked me to come up to the Chief Executive's office. I'm not sure why he wanted me to go to the Chief Executive's Office rather than his, but at this point they had promised I didn't have to talk to David, and so it didn't feel good to be summoned to his office. Too many times that had happened and he had just shouted at me. I wasn't keen on that happening again.

But to my surprise, some sort of self-protection mechanism finally kicked in. I found myself uttering the words "no, why don't you come down here?". Something about the situation was just very odd. And I was still reeling about the meeting the day before. My instincts kicked in. If it was going to get shitty, I'd rather be in my safe space with my team outside the door.

But that wasn't his plan. I think he was hoping that another heavier threat would result in me backing down and accepting his pay off.

He started getting angry on the phone, demanding that I come upstairs immediately. I asked what it was about I suggested if it was urgent couldn't we talk about it on the phone? or couldn't he come down?

I can't remember exactly what he said next because it was just so surreal, but he basically lost his temper.

He said he had thought about it, and if I wasn't going to go settle, take the money and sign a non disclosure agreement, he felt he needed to suspend me on the spot for all the things he'd heard about me, and that I had to leave the building right now.

Shocked, I asked him what exactly he was suspending me for.

He got all woolly and flustered and avoided the question.

He said that he would write me a letter to tell me, but that I had to get out now, and take my stuff and not talk to anyone.

I probably would have burst into tears had the shock been less.

I will admit here that I didn't do what Glenn had told me, my team could see the look on my face and they were worried. I couldn't just walk out and not tell them what had happened, they would be stuck in a loop of not knowing what on earth, it would be awful for them. I explained that I had been suspended, that they were all fine, and that I would be fine, and that I couldn't speak to them, but they were fabulous, and they would be able to run things without me, and I would be OK. And I walked out into the sunshine.

I remember the oddness of the moment. I left the good girl in that building. I did not feel shame or fear at that moment (although I got some of that later, the good girl hangs on and comes back to haunt you at times) I just felt overwhelming relief. I knew deep down that I hadn't done anything to deserve this, that this was a reaction to me challenging them. But in hindsight, I also felt an overwhelming relief that I was safe.

That's what I felt that day, as I walked down the hill in the sunshine to my car. I felt that I was free.

They couldn't hurt me anymore.

I was on suspension, on full pay, for fourteen months.

You may think that sounds fabulous. But of course, I didn't know it would be that long, and every day I wondered what would happen next.

Once your employer gets this weird, anything is possible right? I genuinely wondered whether someone would try to physically threaten me, it certainly wouldn't be the first time. There was that time I was on jury service and ended up as the foreman, and we ended up convicting a notorious gang leader for attempted murder and I had to be sneaked out of the back of the court by the police for my safety as he kicked off when I said he was guilty and started shouting and screaming about "kangaroo courts" and threatening me and my family... but well that is another story....

No, I didn't really think I was physically in danger, but I wasn't sure, and it felt as if I was in physical danger. There was that disconnect between what my body was telling me and what my logical brain was telling me.

Whilst I was on suspension, ENC's lawyers offered me a promotion (but in another organisation), offered a redundancy payout, offered various payments to leave, and threatened that if I didn't leave, drop all my complaints and sign a non-disclosure agreement then I would never work in HR ever again.

They also attempted mediation, but David Oliver attended then refused to talk to me and the mediation was cancelled. I don't think he had the guts to face me, and although I saw him from a distance that day, I've never seen him since...

After fourteen months I think they finally realised that I wasn't going to resign and sign a non-disclosure agreement or go away, so they invited me to attend a disciplinary hearing instead, immediately after I said I was struggling with my mental health too much to come in to have a meeting about the promotion they were offering me.

Two weeks before the Disciplinary Hearing, in an email, still unclear what exactly I was being accused of, I asked Glenn to confirm what the allegations were. Grumpy, he emailed me back, and I quote:

Email from Glenn Hammons dated 15th April 2019[39]

Hi Aime

In response to your question. I confirm that the allegation on page 29 headed "AA communicated false remarks about what had been said by the authority's Chief Executive at a confidential session off Personal Sub Committee" is included within the allegations against you and is covered under paragraph 3.1 of the disciplinary invite letter.

The allegations within the disciplinary invite letter make abundantly clear the allegations that are being presided against you. On that basis, I do not believe that it is necessary to further clarify the allegations against you.

Regards

Glenn

The first hearing only lasted a few hours, because it became clear that things were in a bit more of a mess than Glenn had wanted to admit. This despite the fact I had been on suspension for more than a year.

I don't think Glenn had got much HR advice up till that point, but he had someone with him for the hearing. It became apparent during the hearing, that it wasn't at all clear what I had been accused of, or what the allegations were. After a couple of hours they decided to end the hearing and regroup.

Bearing in mind, the investigation had been concluded, and the report written nine months before the disciplinary hearing, and I'd asked for clarity about the allegations and been told I didn't need any.

On first May 2019 I got an email listing twelve allegations that were to be dropped because there was no case to answer or they weren't misconduct issues. Including the one about "communicating false remarks about David Oliver".

On twentieth May I received a letter confirming that more allegations were dropped.

After a couple of months of sorting themselves out, they rearranged another hearing. They had dropped 92% of the allegations acknowledging that there was no case to answer for them, or they weren't misconduct issues.

Good girls aren't supposed to stick up for themselves. They are supposed to shut up and do as they are told, except when their knowledge and skills are useful to others, then they are allowed to talk.

I had been at ENC for more than eight years, I had aced every test, every appraisal, delivered every target, and achieved things that most people wouldn't have tried including:

- Scored very highly each year in the staff survey (my team always came out in the top 10% of the teams with lots of positive comments).
- Undertaken more than a dozen incredibly difficult dismissals including ill health, poor performance and fraud. All without there being a single appeal, let alone a tribunal (no mean feat). In fact during my 25 year HR career, only two decisions I have ever advised on amongst hundreds, have staff ever appealed, and not a single one has ever even got as far as submitting an ET1 (which is the paperwork that official starts the process of an Employment Tribunal).
- Written and delivered a management training programme for all middle managers.
- Negotiated the removal of company cars from all senior managers, winning praise from both the Trade Union, members and staff because I handled the situation with care and sensitivity (although this was another thing some senior managers including David weren't pleased with - it wasn't

my idea to take their company cars away from them, the money had just run out so the councillors decided to take their cars away, but they still seemed to blame me anyway).

- Recruited to hundreds of posts, handling many personally.
- Negotiated and implemented a new payroll contract and transitioned payroll to a new system without a hitch.
- Re-written every single HR policy to simplify and update them, consulted on them, amended them and went through the process of getting them all approved.
- Dealt with dozens of ill health cases, including several deaths, with one actually being on site.
- Personally supported staff who had gone through the most terrible of situations including a murder, several rapes and the tragedy of miscarriages and children that have died.
- Reduced my budget whilst improving performance.
- Either written and delivered personally or commissioned personally every piece of corporate training at ENC.
- Advised on numerous organisational changes, including TUPE and redundancies, re-organisations and commissioning services out to other providers (including all the contract negotiations).
- Advised the Leader of the Council, Chief Exec, board, Personnel Committee and all managers on every employee relations query and staffing issue they had.
- Run the job evaluation scheme, requiring staff to be trained in the process, dealing with 56 pages for each job, all the panels, and appeals, queries upsets and arguments.
- Set up and chaired numerous interagency groups.
- Created a dashboard to monitor all staffing data in a graphical way. Analysing all the data myself.
- Acted as the police lead for the council on a number of investigations, and on the bi-annual deep dive fraud initiative run by a joint task force of government agencies

to seek out any data breaches and investigate them (which included investigating a number of elected councillors).

- All on a salary of £36,000 and with one HR advisor and a part time administrator, whilst attempting to be a mum of two small kids and be married and have a life.
- All without a single complaint, or concern ever mentioned to me.

In fact, until I was suspended, I'd never had a single complaint made about me in my entire career, and had actually received many letters of commendation, thank you cards, and emails. My team had been interviewed for this witch hunt that was called a disciplinary investigation. They had been incredibly supportive, and one had said I was the best manager they had ever had. This was written off by the investigating officer as being unlikely to be true, because I was their boss, and they probably just felt obliged to say nice things about me.

As I sat in the hotel lobby before the reconvened disciplinary hearing my hands were shaking.

My mental health was all over the place, and I was fighting for my sanity as well as my career. I was on my own. The trade union who I was a member of had deserted me, because the local rep was one of the people who had made an allegation against me.

I wasn't entitled to legal representation.

I wanted to throw up.

But I had taken the tough route and not accepted the payouts, so now I was going to have to go through with this.

Whilst for fourteen months the allegations had been unclear, following some work with an excellent HR person who had been supporting Glenn, they were at least in a sensible and understandable format by this point.

So, what were the allegations?

1. Breaching confidence by passing on confidential information.
2. Raising an equal pay claim that had upset some staff.

3. Being argumentative and confrontational.
4. Creating a negative and hostile working environment that has caused a breakdown in working relationships with the CEO and Senior officers.

I know I hadn't passed on any confidential information, and the other three accusations pretty much boil down to me being a difficult woman and putting in my three complaints.

But let me explain a bit about the timeline. I have put the outcomes to my complaints first in this book, because I made them first. But in fact, at the point I was sitting in my disciplinary hearing, they hadn't started investigations into any of them. They were accusing me of these things without having started any investigations into any of my allegations. They were hoping all along you see that they would never need to investigate, because I would just cave under pressure.

They underestimated my stubbornness.

It wasn't until after I was dismissed, and only after I went to external audit, that there were any investigations.

But if I'm being really fair, I should let you decide whether I was guilty of breaching confidence by passing on confidential information. So let me tell you about the three allegations they made.

What secrets did they think I had shared?

Now there is some irony to this situation, as I didn't share these secrets.

But ENC now has.

By putting them in the disciplinary investigation, and thus the appeal and then taking them to the employment tribunal, they actually shared these secrets far far wider than I had even been accused of.

The paperwork has been read by dozens of people, and tribunal papers and judgements are a matter of public record. They have been read by advisors, and investigators, and staff were questioned about them, lawyers and councillors read them, and then councillors shared details with the press.

These three things were secrets, but they aren't now.

In fact it appears that one of the employees ENC named complained to the Council and the Information Commission, both of whom acknowledged that ENC had breached Data Protection Legislation by including their details in the claim against me.

ENC put the details and the people's names in the documents, and they are included within the court papers, but I'm not going to name names. In fact, I'm going to be a bit woolly. I didn't breach confidentiality then, and I'm not going to now, even if ENC has.

The first accusation was about pregnancy. The story goes like this.

An ex employee, let's call her Jane, called me to ask about a job. She had left ENC almost 7 years before my disciplinary hearing. She wanted to know if her being pregnant meant that she wouldn't be considered for the job.

Of course, I said it didn't make a difference.

Which is true.

But we still didn't shortlist her, but for a very different reason.

What she hadn't known, was that before she resigned, we were about to put her on notice that unless her performance improved, we would dismiss her. She knew she was struggling, and I think she sensed that we weren't happy, which was why she left. Also, to be fair, the role she had applied for would have been a considerable step up for her anyway. So, because of these reasons, we didn't shortlist her.

I didn't hear any more from her.

Two years later, she applied for a more junior role at ENC and I wasn't on the panel or involved in shortlisting, she got the job and came back. I didn't have a problem with this, everyone deserves a second chance, and I hoped she would be very successful in her new role.

Jane had rung me about the role in 2013. She started back at ENC in 2015.

In 2018 the investigating officer looking into my disciplinary allegations, was asked by Glenn Hammons to interview her.

She told this story.

I had apparently told another employee, let's call them Brian, that she was pregnant in 2013.

Brian had then apparently told Gail that Jane was pregnant.

On seeing Jane, Gail congratulated her on being pregnant.

But apparently, as her bump wasn't very clear, and because she had only told six people at ENC that she'd been pregnant, and I was the only one she didn't trust, then I must have told Brian, who told Gail, because that was the only way Gail could possibly have known that she was pregnant, when she met her for lunch.

Yep, slam dunk that one (you may have to re-read it to even try to follow their logic).

I know I didn't tell anyone that Jane was pregnant. To be honest, other than just being supportive and congratulatory, I quickly forgot about it. I was on the shortlisting panel for the role Jane had applied for, and we chose not to shortlist her. But we didn't talk about her pregnancy. We did talk about the fact that she had been underperforming in her previous role and that we needed a really strong person for the role we were appointing to.

Generally, it is considered good practice to investigate any allegations at the time they happen. If you don't, memories get blurry, and it is also fairer to deal with things as they happen. But needing to end my seemingly never-ending suspension, and with me refusing to take a payment and leave, Glenn needed to find something to accuse me of. If they had dropped every allegation with zero proof they would have been left with nothing, so they left this one in, because Jane was happy to go on the record and accuse me of sharing her pregnancy with Brian, even though Brian had not been interviewed, and Gail had seen Jane (who was pregnant) and that Gail had said that Brian had told her, but

Brian hadn't said that I told him. Basically, they were desperate for allegations, and an allegation of a breach of confidence from someone who ran HR sounds pretty serious. They left this one in, because, it was the best allegation they had left...

In the second allegation it is going to be a little difficult to hide the people, but I'll try.

A member of the trade union committee came to me in early 2018 to ask for my advice. Someone close to them had been suspended from work because they had been accused of theft. It was the second time it had happened, but it was for a small amount, and they had meant to pay back the money but had forgotten.

In hindsight, the person coming to me had probably wanted me to tell them that it would all be OK.

But, and I don't always know if this is the right thing to do.

I tend to be a fairly honest person.

I told them that I thought it would be an overreaction to sack them for such a small amount, they might, and it would probably be considered sound at an employment tribunal.

This was not the response they wanted. They stormed out of my office furious with me.

David Oliver had been interviewed at Glenn Hammons' request during my disciplinary investigation and had stated that I had told him that the person who had been accused of theft had been sacked.

I didn't. I wouldn't have shared such information with anyone anyway. But I wasn't talking to David and did everything I could to avoid him. To suggest that I had shared something when we were just chatting, even though he had promised not to talk to me because of my bullying allegation was basically absurd.

Below is an exact transcript of what he said as accepted by ENC (they recorded the hearing, and I had this bit transcribed professionally from the audio, and they accepted that this was an accurate verbatim transcript of what happened during the hearing). By the way exact transcripts are always a bit odd to read, people don't talk in the same way they write, so exact transcripts always read a little oddly. I've changed the name of the employee to X and the friend to Y to protect their confidentiality, but they are listed in all the ENC paperwork.[39]

AA....................Okay, first question. Can you give me a few more details about what the allegation regarding X's Y is?

DO ....Not sure I've got anything to answer beyond what's in here really. That was about you telling me that he had been sacked from his job, which wasn't something that I was aware of or needed to know. It felt to me like it was very much a private matter. Not something I needed to be aware of at all really.

AA ....Can you give a bit more context about when you think I told you, where you think I told you?

DO....................No I couldn't give you the dates and times on that. It would have been at a meeting in my office I would imagine, but I can't give you the date.

AA....................Okay, so you don't think I should have told you. What was your initial response to me?

DO ....I can't remember.

AA....................OK. Did you think it was serious?

DO....................I thought it was unprofessional. I wouldn't say I thought it was serious because I know X well enough and I've got a good enough relationship with X to know that it's the kind of thing X wouldn't be upset about me knowing and X might have wanted to tell me themself. But I didn't feel as it was appropriate for you to share that with me, or with anybody else in fact. If your intention was to make me aware that X was going through a difficult personal issue that might've affected their work or there relationship in some way but my feeling was that you could have done that simply by saying "X's got some personal stuff going on, just so that you're aware they might be different". I didn't feel like it was necessary or appropriate to give me that level of personal detail about what was going on in their family.

AA....................The reasons I'm questioning when and exactly what, is that from my recollection she never told me that he was dismissed. She told me some other details earlier on in the process because she asked for my advice.

AA.................... Is it possible that your memory is...

DO....................laughs

AA....................I'm trying to be subtle and polite...

DO....................There's no need to be polite. It is a well known fact that my memory is not the best.

AA....................And I'm not...I believe that you're an honest person, but you remember things inaccurately sometimes. Could that be

DO....................All I can say is that is my recollection of that. If you hadn't told me that, I don't know how I would've known.

AA....................You just said that you were quite friendly with X plus in your statement you said you talked about it afterwards, in fact, they state that you went and told her that I told

DO.................... didn't go and tell her. I imagine you know I have fairly frequent meetings with X.

AA....................I don't mean you walk down straight away, I meant you told her at some point that I had apparently disclosed this information.

DO....................Yea, I dare say that was they sequence of events, you told me then I told her.

AA....................Dare say, or actually remember?

DO....................Yea well you told me and then I told her. Yes that was the sequence of events. But, exactly when that happened I couldn't be more specific.

AA....................So obviously you're the chief exec, you're three levels above me and have a fair amount of power and authority in the organisation, so you could have taken all sorts of actions if you said you didn't feel as if I should have told you. You've said that it wasn't potentially that serious but you could have taken actions. You could have, it's extreme but you could have suspended me, you could have taken disciplinary action, you could have raised it at an appraisal, you could have raised it in a management meeting, you could have raised it in a capability. You didn't raise it in any of those things.

DO....................True

HR....................What's the question Aime, sorry.

AA....................Did you raise it in any format with me? Did you raise it even just in an aside?

DO....................Not that I remember no.

Not exactly the clearest I've ever been. I knew I hadn't told him, but I was trying not to call him a liar directly. I was trying to get him to acknowledge that maybe he had been mistaken. I was trying to suggest that surely if I had told him he would have taken action immediately, and the fact that he hadn't suggests that maybe that wasn't how he learnt the information. It was all very odd. Because he said it wasn't very serious, and that he probably would have been told anyway, and that he couldn't remember the details. He even acknowledged that he didn't have a good memory. And of course, he keeps interrupting me. But like the last allegation, they didn't have much to go on, so this was as good as it got. The Chief Executive accused me of doing something, and he was believed, even though I had accused him of bullying, wasn't talking to him, he had a terrible memory he was good friends with the person who might have told him another way. But he was believed, and I wasn't.

Going to a few pages ahead in the transcript, I wanted to ask him why there weren't any file notes about this "alleged incident" if DO didn't have a good memory, surely, he would have made a note? There was no note of this conversation, or email or document provided at any point (but of course that is not odd, because why would there be a record of a conversation that never happened?). Any lawyers or scientists amongst you know that it is very difficult to prove something didn't happen. Because of course if something didn't happen then there is no evidence. The expectation is that if something did happen then there would be evidence. This was the point I was trying to make. David, didn't have a good memory, there were no notes, nothing happened afterwards, he couldn't remember the event (because it didn't happen). He just assumed that it must have happened, because how else could he have known, even though he admitted he was friends with the person and they talked to him a lot about such things...

AA.....................It's just normal, if someone has an allegation and someone has a file note it is considered usually evidence

DO ....Yea, I don't know what happened to those notes.

So, to summarise David's version of what happened: At some point, despite the fact that I don't get on with David at all, and think he is a bully; I wandered up to speak to him to tell him a personal piece of information for no apparent reason about someone I knew he was friends with. He didn't make a note, or if he did make a note that note disappeared. He doesn't remember what he said or did about my alleged comment, or when it happened, or exactly what was said. But he didn't think it was very serious, and he agrees he didn't do anything about it. He didn't tell me I shouldn't have said it or bring it up in a one to one when he managed me, or suspend me, or any other action. In fact, nothing happened until I was suspended and he was interviewed six months later, then after talking to his friend about it several times, he's absolutely sure it happened. Despite the fact he admits, and everyone knows he doesn't have a good memory. And he reported it after I had put in a bullying complaint against him, and an equal pay claim and a whilstleblowing allegation that was about him.

Or my version of events, X did tell me about the case. But I didn't talk to David about it at all. He did talk to X about the situation, and they explained that they had had a conversation with me about it, but they were angry because I had said that it was probably a justifiable suspension. Y was then dismissed, which I didn't know anything about until I read it in the paperwork. X asked if I had ever mentioned it to him and feeling defensive and not having much else to blame me for, his subconscious cobbled together that the only thing that could have possibly happened was that I told him, and that that should be gross misconduct.

I'll let you decide what you think happened. But Glenn had

already decided that it was all my fault.

According to X I (who also made a statement) I was also "battling against the council for what might only be seen as her own agenda. AA appears to be looking for a fight with ENC...there is a lack of trust in AA from myself and my trade union. There needs to be trust in the HR Manager and it is just not there"

I'm assuming that they were referring to my complaints.

The most senior member of the Trade Union, the branch chair, didn't appear to agree with this assessment. Quoting from his statement he said[40]

> *"Personally, I have never had an issue with AA in respect of any alleged breach of confidentiality on her part. I am aware of suggestions that she may have but that is hearsay and not my direct experience of her.*
>
> *I have no recollection that AA as alleged made inappropriate comments about the employment status of Z. There may have been a comment that Z was absent from the authority, but no reasons were divulged as far as I can recall.*
>
> *I can recall that on one occasion AA abruptly left a meeting involve trade unions and the CEX in some sort of huff and felt it odd at the time that AA had left her boss to continue the meeting without HR support. This may have even about job evaluation, but I cannot be sure.*
>
> *My own relationship with her is on the whole good but aware of the opinions and experience others have had with AA I am circumspect in what I might divulge go her. I have however, noticed for a while that certain issues have dragged on in terms of any resolution or improvement such as job evaluation or recruitment processes and that log James are not addressed. JE has been inconsistent in terms of the approach to it by HR and cases take some time to be resolved.*
>
> *I have a business and police background and I find it difficult to understand why issues that need addressing*

take so long or that little progress is made. It is difficult to ascertain whether this is solely down to AA are whether she is under some form of constraint from above. The authority has been through some challenging times especially in respect of CMT issues, so it hasn't been easy for AA working here."

If you were wondering, CMT was the corporate management team, essentially the board. And Z, well that brings us to the final secret I had supposedly shared.

I wasn't the first person to raise a formal complaint about David Oliver being a bully. Z did so first. David asked me to advise and sort out the situation. I refused to get involved. I couldn't with all due conscience or professionalism get involved in what they wanted to do (which was pressure her to drop her claims).

They got external advice. Z went off sick and eventually put in a grievance against David Oliver and others (including politicians). She then also put in an employment tribunal claim.

The first stage of an employment tribunal is to go through ACAS, then you need to write what is called an ET1 which is your grounds of action. Then the ET1 is sent to your employer who has 28 days to submit an ET3, which is the legal response to the allegations. It is a point of natural justice that everyone should know what the allegations are and should be allowed to respond to them.

One day just before Christmas, just before I put in my claims, the ET1 for Z arrived on my desk. It had gone round the houses before it had got to me, and everyone knew that Z was not at work. The ET1 hadn't had a name on it, so the post room had opened the envelope and it had apparently gone via several people to work out what it was before they realised and gave it to me. I checked the date that it needed to be returned (tight timescale remember, and noted that two weeks had already elapsed) and passed it up to the Monitoring Officer, the person who has the legal responsibility at any local authority. Usually a lawyer, but in ENC's case an experienced manager, but who was not a lawyer.

I didn't need to read the ET1 because Z had phoned me to tell me what was happening. In fact, they had phoned me several times, very upset. And also, to ask me to be a witness on their behalf. I said that I didn't want to get involved as such but would obviously be a witness to anything that had happened and would tell the truth, including some rather unpleasant happenings. I don't want to go into this here, because as I've said it isn't my story.

Z never came back to work, and I didn't know exactly what had happened. I just saw the email saying they weren't coming back. But as the person who verifies payroll (I explained a bit about that earlier), I have to check payroll each month, and always run a report that sorts by amount. It allows me to check that any silly errors like putting in an extra zero on someone's salary and taking them from a £40,000 annual salary to a £400,000 annual salary haven't happened. A large settlement was always going to instantly come out on top. I wasn't involved in arranging the deal and I was never told the exact details, but I guessed that a settlement had been agreed.

There are four ways to end an employment contract. You can resign and end the contract yourself. Your employer can end your contract (through redundancy or dismissal). Your contract can run out (a fixed term contract), or it can be ended through mutual agreement through a process that used to be called a compromise agreement but is now called a settlement agreement. I'm not a big fan, especially in the public sector, as they nearly always include NDAs (non-disclosure agreements, or gag clauses as they are more colloquially known).

But they get used more than you might imagine.

The Taxpayers Alliance undertook a piece of research that covers this period asking all local authorities what they had spent on settlement agreements[41] using Freedom of Information legislation.

If you are interested, you can click on the link embedded in their research and find out how much your council spent.

Between 2016 and 2019 Local Councils in the UK signed 6,980 settlement agreements and paid out over £98 million of taxpayers money.

The highest settlement agreement was £195,463 at Stoke-On-

Trent and they also had the highest number of settlements.45 authorities reported spending zero on settlement agreements. It can be done.

Without giving you the exact amount, let's just say that the payout at ENC given to Z would have put it in the top 10% of all settlements made across local authorities over that period.

It was not a small amount of money.

I was accused of sharing details of this "termination agreement" as they called it in the paperwork.

Again, the irony is, that I didn't tell anyone, but ENC told lots of people. Employee Z's name is all over the paperwork, as are details of this situation, including in the public domain in the tribunal paperwork. Which is a little odd, as both parties tend to agree not to discuss with anyone the existence of a settlement agreement

And if you go back to the Chair of the Trade Union's statement. He says and I quote...

"I have no recollection that AA as alleged made inappropriate comments about the employment status of Z. There may have been a comment that Z was absent from the authority, but no reasons were divulged as far as I can recall."

We try to avoid leading questions during an investigation.

We don't say "did you see Jane stealing a handbag from Marks and Spencers?" Because the evidence is that many people will say yes, even if Jane was never in Marks and Spencers. It taints the validity of the answer.

Instead, we might say. Did you see anything odd or illegal in Marks and Spencers today?

They might say, no, or yes I saw Jane steal a wallet, or that they saw a woman steal a handbag. You see there are lots of elements to this phrase. They may well have seen a handbag being stolen, but didn't know who it was, but when given Jane's name, might have thought, yes, it was probably Jane.

So, the trade union rep states that he had no recollection that I made inappropriate comments about the employment status of Z.

So, what question, elicits that kind of response?

It would have needed to have included the person's name, and the suggestion that I had said something illicit about Z and their employment status. So the question was probably

"Did Aime tell you anything inappropriate about Z's employment status?"

Or maybe they even asked the more direct

"Did Aime tell you about Z's termination agreement?" (the phrase termination agreement in relation to Z is all over the paperwork, despite the fact that there is essentially no such thing as a termination agreement, either you terminate, or someone settles, no-one agrees to being terminated).

Ask enough people that question, leave it 14 months before you have the hearing, and you've started your very own rumour about Z ...

Because if the trade union chair above had been asked, is there anything you'd like to tell me about Aime? He'd have just said no wouldn't he? Not "I have no recollection that AA has alleged made inappropriate comments about the employment status of Z".

And that's why we usually commission experts to do complex disciplinary investigations. But in this case, Glenn Hammons had appointed an ex-Geography teacher, with no HR qualifications and only about a year working in HR. Side bar here. I did A level Geography, and I now do lots of great work with my ex-Geography teacher at the Coopers. This isn't a criticism of Geography teachers, I love Geography, and my teachers were AMAZING. But they are great Geography teachers, not HR experts...

It was never stated exactly what I was supposed to have told whom about the termination agreement, just that I had discussed it. That is clear then... start a rumour, which other people had already known about, then ask lots of loaded questions... and well then, even though no-one actually says that I've told them anything, you've got a slam dunk case...

But again, they knew it was a weak argument, but it was the only one they had...so they were prepared to risk being sued about breaching the very agreement they signed with employee Z...

That's it, that is the three allegations that I breached confidentiality

1. Apparently telling someone, who told someone else who then noticed that someone was pregnant but didn't complain about it until six years later when asked, and knew it was me because I was the only person of the six she had told that she didn't trust.
2. David Oliver, who I had put in a bullying complaint and whistleblowing complaint about, who didn't really remember what happened was certain I had told him something confidential, even though we weren't talking.
3. Me apparently talking about a hush hush settlement agreement for a large-scale amount, that I wasn't involved with, which no-one said I had told them anything specific about, but a few people knew about, so it must have been me that told them...

Clearly bang to rights. I'm obviously a bad 'un.

Ah but there was something else wasn't there.

I had also been accused of being argumentative and confrontational and creating a negative and hostile working environment that has caused a breakdown in working relationships with the CEO and Senior officers.

Almost all of the evidence for this was dropped, including the allegation by David Oliver (as mentioned in Glenn's email above) that I had been apparently

"communicated false remarks about what had been said by the authority's Chief Executive at a confidential session of Personnel Sub Committee"

They dropped this allegation because Personnel Sub Committee has lots of attendees and is minuted. And they couldn't find any evidence of the allegation from the attendees or in the minutes.

And they dropped the allegation about unfairly suggesting that a senior manager should have gone through a more thorough recruitment process. Because I suspect the HR expert explained that it generally wasn't considered to be OK for a hearing officer to hear claims about themselves... (because the allegation was about me challenging Glenn's recruitment process and daring to suggest that there should have been an advert and references should have been sought, and that he shouldn't have just been slotted into the role).

And by the way, if some of this has been difficult to follow, then don't feel too bad, it has given me numerous headaches. When I do disciplinary investigations they are clear and well evidenced. In fact, I have done several recently where the lawyers involved have said that they have been the best investigations they have ever seen in their whole careers. I've tried to explain a confusing mess. But I can only do so much...

I was dismissed on 14th June 2019 by Glenn Hammons without my job evaluation claims being investigated, without my whistleblowing allegations being investigated, and without my bullying allegations against David Oliver being investigated (all of that came later).

One of the reasons cited in my dismissal letter was the way in which I brought my equal pay claim. Apparently and I quote from my dismissal letter , 41

"some individuals were "cross" and "furious "and upset with you for doing this... therefore this is an example of your conduct detrimentally impacting on working relationships, a serious breach of trust and confidence,"

I'll accept that me raising an equal pay claim upset some people. That was not my intention, and for that I am sorry.

But hold on a second.

Basically part of the reason I was sacked was people didn't like that I had raised an equal pay claim. How desperate do you have to be to actual type in a dismissal letter that the reason for misconduct you are relying on is to do with an equal pay claim?

This would all be very funny. If it wasn't my life.

I mean at least this isn't Salem, or even the witch hunt in the UK during the English Civil War. I mean let's be honest, I would have been burnt to death then.

It really isn't funny is it.

It might be illegal to burn difficult women today, but well, we still aren't treated fairly.

But maybe I needed this to happen.

Maybe this is the best thing that could have happened.

I was no longer even pretending to be a good girl.

I was becoming a free woman.

I was starting to realise that there was nothing wrong with me, I was just working for the wrong people.

The seeds of setting up a trade union that would stand beside men and women who had been accused, and fight for their rights, and be there with them was sparked during my own experiences.

I don't want anyone ever to have to go through what I did alone ever again.

And I will use every last ounce of my strength and wit to fight for them to be treated fairly.

Which is why I set up the HR and Workers Trade Union. A Trade Union for people who aren't a member of a trade union but find themselves in a difficult situation. We are a pay as you go trade union who fights for the underdog and the unfairly treated. We are a trade union of last resort for most.

So now you can see my why, I can tell you how I found a way to start healing, and what I did next.

You didn't think I just set up a trade union did you?

But before I could truly fly, I needed to heal a little. And that healing came from some very unexpected sources...

PART THREE:
The Recovery

Chapter 9
A surprising source of loveliness

So, my complaints had been ignored, my reality had been denied, and I'd been sacked. My mental health and self-worth were pretty low.

I needed to find myself again, I needed to start again, I needed to find out what I was going to do with my life.

I booked an all-women physical challenge to spend ten days trekking in China with a group of strangers. Not the most obvious solution, but actually, in hindsight a pretty effective one.

It was going to be physically demanding, as the trek was for charity and we were hiking every day up and along the Great Wall of China. Not something that I traditionally enjoy doing.

If someone had told me that I was going to spend the first trek climbing steps for more than two hours just to get on to the Great Wall of China, I probably wouldn't have gone.

To be honest, I probably shouldn't have gone. I wasn't fit enough, I was hurting emotionally, my pride was hurt.

But the training took my mind off things. I had planned to go alone. But my mum wanted to come too. She was a little worried that she wouldn't be up to it, but although she was 70 at the time, she's fitter and tougher than me, so I was like, let's do it.

I don't remember much of the trip. But I do remember the feeling of starting afresh, of spending ten days with women who didn't know me, or my story.

I was by far the worst in the group physically, but everyone was kind. The group was split into four teams and given challenges. The leader told me afterwards that they do this with most groups, but most groups kind of refuse or don't want to do it. Not our four groups, we really leant into it. Come up with an expressive dance to communicate how you feel about China - done! Find a way to communicate the name of your group without saying it - absolutely. And because our phones didn't work and we were in the middle of nowhere without any wifi and trekking all day, we got to know each other. We bonded; it was lovely.

Mum was worried that as the oldest, she wouldn't really be accepted. But she was, and to be honest, most people tended to call her Mum, partly because there was another Linda, but also because well that's what I called her. Away from Dad, away from her identity in the UK as teacher and Granny and Mum, she rediscovered her silly naughty side. By the time we reached Beijing she had become the naughty one of the group. Exhausted I went to bed, when I saw the videos the next day a small group had gone to karaoke and there was video of Mum standing on a table dancing.

There are many stories I could tell of that trip, of the moments of awe standing in very rural China on top of the wall, of our adventures and sightseeing in Beijing, of what I learnt about the Chinese culture. The main screen on my phone is still a picture I took from the wall out into the forest, it calms me and reminds me that however crazy my day is, however messed up geopolitics are, the world always has the capacity to charm, and amaze me with its wonders. That trip started my sense of healing, and I remembered a little bit of who I was, but I still had to come home.

When I got home, I had no job, no income, and no idea what to do next. I knew I had skills, but I didn't really know how to use them, and I had no idea about business, or social media, or marketing or sales. But I knew that my future wasn't in Public Sector HR, at least not straight away. I needed a fresh start, and I couldn't bear to work for one boss. The whole process had been traumatic, and I needed to find a way to work with different people, so that no one could control my working life totally in the way David Oliver had.

I went to a networking meeting. It was in Louisa's in Market Harborough. A lovely unique space with sofas and light and brunch and cocktails. I went to a Mums in Business Association Networking event. A space only for women, where children were encouraged to come too. Where we sat in a circle and talked a little about ourselves and then well just got to know each other.

And the universe sent me a little luck. In that room that day there were three people who would have an amazing impact on my life going forward, and I would become friends with. By this point Mums in Business was an international networking company with 100s of events happening all over the world. The person who was supposed to run the event that day had had to rush her daughter to hospital with appendicitis, and as it was close to where it all started, the CEO Estelle Keeber had stepped in to cover the event. I had a chat with Estelle afterwards, and MIB became my first client. I helped them deal with all their staffing issues and did some coaching for their top team. It was an amazing journey, and I loved every minute, especially having to research HR rules across the world (the legal structures are surprisingly different in different countries, did you know for example that some countries in the Middle East for example don't essentially have the structures to be self-employed? In all US states except Montana, workers are considered by default to be at-will employees, meaning that they may be fired at any time without cause (one of the reasons most US employees never take more than a few days holiday at a time in case they get back to find they have been replaced), and in Norway employees have a right to remain in their posts until the courts have made a decision about whether their proposed termination is legal!).

Estelle and I are as different as chalk and cheese. We are different in almost every way you can imagine, from our backgrounds, to how we look, to the classes we were born into, to our education, to the way we do things. But we have the same values. We would never have met when we were teenagers, and if we had we wouldn't have been friends. But now, well we are good friends, and we help each other. Because our different backgrounds mean we have different perspectives and different skill sets that are hugely complimentary.

Unfortunately, MIBA didn't last as an organisation, and there is a fascinating story about that, but it isn't mine to tell, so for now, let me just say I am team Estelle. I am so lucky that she trusted me to take me on when I was feeling so low, and to believe in me when I didn't believe in myself.

Barbara Von Ow Hulme and Lindsey were also both at that meeting. Lindsey and I would go onto be firm friends, and Barbara invited me to another networking group. The Leicester Business Network that she ran. LBN no longer exists because Barbara is focusing on her other businesses, but there I met so many other amazing people, mates and fabulous friends, including Claire Flinders, Marie Perry and Mairi Taylor.

My ex-husband once asked me why I was going to networking meetings. What was my goal, what was I going to get out of it, what was my return on investment, was it a valid use of my time?

And that is a typical approach for some people, and it is a useful one that can work. But for me I was just trying to find my feet. I had no idea what I was doing, but I knew that I wasn't going to create a whole new career for myself sitting in my office staring at my computer screen. I needed to explore and talk to people and find out what this new world was like.

At the beginning I had more time than I had products or clients. It was a delicious time, where I could arrange two one to one meetings before a networking meeting that covered lunch time, and two afterwards and basically spend all day talking to people.

Having worked predominantly in the public sector, and having been treated quite harshly, I expected the small business world to be brutal and greedy.

But it wasn't, people were generous with their time and their expertise, and they helped me and looked after me.

I bumped into Kelly Trickett at another MIBA meeting in Loughborough. She was the first HR small business owner I bumped into, and I liked her from the first moment we met. Again, she had similar values to me and was incredibly skilled at what she did. She offered to help me and even gave me for free the employee staff book she had written and told me I could sell it on.

What?

How generous is that?

I couldn't afford to pay her right then, but I vowed to pay the favour back in kind. As our business grew, we went in slightly different ways. I love doing the big, complicated one off pieces of work, and then often I get offered jobs at the end, as HR Manager or HR Director or just to come in and deliver all their HR on a contract basis. I tried this a couple of times, and it kind of worked for a bit, but it wasn't what I wanted to do. I like to do the really tough stuff, and prefer to help many clients. So when some clients asked me to support them with all their HR I paid that debt back and introduced them to Kelly (because I knew she would be able to deliver as well as I could, probably better with the day to day stuff). And sometimes if she has a really complicated case, she isn't sure about, she gives me a call. But to be honest, all I tend to do is reassure her that she is on the right track. I haven't seen Kelly for ages, but I see on social media her company growing and taking on staff and being successful, and I smile, quite frankly it couldn't have happened to a more wonderful and capable HR professional.

I also joined the CIPD committee for Leicestershire. That was great fun, until I got annoyed with the CIPD head office... but well, as they say, that is another story...

But again, I got to spend some time with some amazing people. Joy Collins runs an amazing Leicestershire HR group that supports standalone HR practitioners and practitioners that support many businesses, I loved that group, and was incredibly grateful that they listened to some of my ideas and allowed me to try out the idea of the Trade Union with them - which they were all incredibly supportive of. And it meant that I got to meet the amazing Rhiannon Stafford too (still love watching what she is up to - love the work she does and the way she thinks). Then when I'd taken on a big contract that I'd managed to sell but didn't actually have the capacity to deliver, the amazing Maureen Tallis stepped in to help me out. An experienced HR Director who I knew I could trust, I just let her get on with it - the client absolutely loved her, and well she did me a solid!

Leicestershire has a really thriving business networking community, and I have been lucky enough to be part of two other amazing groups, both female led. Women that Connect is a one of a kind monthly networking group, led by the fabulous Debbie Heron, and then there is the amazing Love Biz where I met both Payal Walker and Sandra Wiggins. When you meet some people you just feel that you have known them for a lifetime, and I feel that way about both Payal and Sandra. They have been cooking up things for a while, and I am really looking forward to attending their launch session of Women on Boards at the House of Lords later this year. I'm excited to find out how their collaboration with the UN's UK Women develops. I feel so incredibly fortunate to have met such amazing people, and to have found so much friendship, collaboration and resonance between what we do.

I could keep talking about the amazing people I met through networking... but, this is meant to be one book not twelve, so I'd better stop there, but I can't finish this chapter without talking about my business partners Kelly, Kelly and Clare.

I have spent a lot of time managing large teams, recruiting, and dealing with conflict, and I've become pretty good at reading people. In the later chapter about EMDT you will hear the story of me creating a psychometric test and eventually turning it into a product which we now sell to support entrepreneurs tap into their best selves. But here I'm going to talk about the three amazing businesswomen who are my business partners.

One of the problems any entrepreneur comes across is funding to grow. It's a circular problem, to get more customers and sell more you have to do more, which requires time and expertise (often not your own, such as someone to do the accounts, someone to help with marketing, someone to help with graphics etc). But how do you afford to pay people to do the work that will allow you to grow?

Well with the Kickstart scheme (more about that later) I'd been lucky and managed to sell enough to scale to a team of 10 quickly (albeit temporarily) because I had sold enough personally to make this work, and with Ninja HR doing general HR work, I'd also managed to sell enough to grow the team (again, more later). With the EMDT I'd managed to test and build a prototype using profits from Kickstart and Ninja HR but I had started to run out of money and needed some fresh capital to push it further. But I didn't want to borrow money or sell ownership as I'd by now seen too many companies be forced to do what the new owners or the banks wanted to make money, not follow their own values.

I had a problem.

But I also had some amazing friends.

Kelly Mayne can code anything. A self-taught coder, she loves it. The more complex the better. I got a few costings for the next stage of EMDT and they were all £50,000 to £100,000 and I wasn't convinced that they had the skills or understanding to actually deliver. But I knew Kelly could do it because I've seen what she could do in the past, and that she loves it. Where most people look a bit white when I tell them what I want, she just rubs her hands and says, can I start now? She's the only person I have ever met who works faster than I do, and where I actually have to slow things down, because she gets so excited about starting the work.

Clare McCabe is a time-served Graphic Designer. Sure, she can do Canva and teaches courses on it, but she is old school - she can actually draw. She is also often considered the Aime whisperer, because she can take my crazy ideas and envision them. She was the one who heckled one of my first presentations and came up with the Ninja HR name, and the logo. She is amazing at everything graphics based, but her real skill is in publishing. She takes people like me with no expertise and just the desire to write and helps us go through all the stages.

And then there is the lovely Kelly Allen, of Admin Assassin. I get all excited about ideas, and I can do the boring stuff, like admin, but I don't like to, and I'll leave it till the last minute. But I've worked with loads of admin people and usually they haven't got the confidence to tell me off or chase me or remind me I'm not making any bloody sense. Kelly, however, has a rare and valuable skill. Also, where she hates the messy bit I love; she loves the organised bit which I hate. And if I'm too soft, Kelly will defend me to the ends of the universe. Seriously, I think if someone actually threatened me in a physical fight she might actually punch them.

They are all bloody amazing, and their skills are just what I needed, so I decided to do something unusual in this crazy world and live my values.

I've made rather a big deal of Equal Pay. We live in a world where usually the ideas and leadership person who starts things off earns more than the incredibly organised person behind the scenes, and often a LOT more.

But well, why not be the change in the world that I want to see.

(Plus I'd run out of money).

So I rang all three of them separately with a crazy idea...

If I set up a new company, and sell all my intellectual property to it for £1, then give all four of us equal shares in the company, will you help me build a company together? We will all put our time in for free now, but whatever successes we have, we will share the profits equally, both as we go, and if we ever sell the company, we will have 25% of the money each.

Kelly Allen said yes before I even explained what I was going to do. She had been key in both the Kickstart adventure and the HRWTU and just enjoyed working with me, I think.

Kelly Mayne loved the idea of coding it but being able to share the profits, rather than coding for someone else who would make a fortune from her work.

And well Clare's my mate and seems to put up with me, so she said yes too, and I think she also believes in what I can do, and my crazy ideas.

The collaborative team that is **Shevolution Ltd** was born, with the wonderful support of Coach and friend Sandra Whiles.

When I told a few people, some thought I was mad. Why give away so much?

Well 100% of nothing is still nothing.

And 25% of a successful business, is still more than 100% of nothing.

Plus, I'd rather do it with friends.

The journey is fun.

I want to be on a beach somewhere celebrating our successes in a few year's time with far too many cocktails.

But I don't want to be on a beach on my own - that wouldn't be much fun.

Command and control is dead as a model whether you like it or not.

Inspire and engage is where it's at.

And I need them all, not just because I need their skills (which I do, they are all bloody amazing, and I'm just really, really lucky they don't understand how amazing they are otherwise they might not have signed up for this crazy journey with me!), I need their support.

We have planned the company so that there is time for us all to vary how much work we need to do and when, including me. When I get overwhelmed and need to retreat, they look after me.

We have a weekly meeting, we'd agreed we didn't need to do much yesterday, because everything was on track, but we met anyway, to share our stories from the week, to be there for each other. Because it isn't just about being a team, it is about being friends, and catching up makes us all feel good. It can be lonely running your own small business, but running one with your friends is great fun.

And what did we do with our first profits? We spent all day in the Tarot Lounge in Hinckley, we had breakfast and lunch and many many cocktails, we talked about life and loves and Star Trek and just generally enjoyed each other's company.

It has been impossible to mention everyone because my life has been touched by so many amazing business owners, and I don't want this to turn into a list.

To all the lovely people I've met, who have been kind to me, and helped me and believed in me, that have helped me heal all the hurt and trauma I experienced. I owe you everything. You helped me to recover and find a way forward to a better future. I will forever be grateful, and well you have my phone details, if you ever need a favour, you know I'm there for you .... the lovely businesspeople I have met have been my surprising source of loveliness, and I have made so many friends. The strange thing is that I would never have met any of these amazing people if I hadn't been sacked, because I would have moved onto another similar job in a similar organisation. It may have been painful, but it was a diversion that helped created a path to a life where I could truly be happy and free.

Chapter 10
Naughty girls, sex parties, divorce and Bumble

Feel free to miss this chapter if you are easily shocked (or you are my parents).

I'm not going to hold back.

You have been warned.

Good girls are not supposed to be dirty.

Good girls are not supposed to like sex, have strong libidos, be explorative and well enjoy themselves.

I guess good girls are supposed to fall in love and kind of just kind of demurely put off sex until marriage and even then, not really enjoy it but do it because it pleases their husbands, and they want children.

The paradox of the society we live in is that it kind of wants us to be good girls, but really really wants the naughty girl in the bedroom. We live in a world where women are sexualised as objects all the time, yet we are not supposed to be sexual ourselves.

And naughty girls are supposed to want to dress a certain way and want to do everything men want, at all times.

When I decided to take a stance at work, I guess it was inevitable that sooner or later my marriage would come to an end.

Not because my ex-husband wasn't supportive of what I did at work, in fact he was. He is a strong feminist, the brightest man I've ever met, a fabulous dad and literally saves lives as a paramedic after getting fed up being a senior civil servant. He also happened to play Tennis for GB and won the British Grass Court over 45's Championships at Wimbledon a couple of years ago. We always co-parented. We both worked part time, we both got up in the middle of the night. My ex-husband is a great guy.

I tried to do the whole wifey thing; I really did. Hell, we moved to a five bedroom detached house in a village in Leicestershire, had two children and a dog. I couldn't quite bear to join the PTA, but I did become a school governor, and I learnt to bake and took the girls to tennis lessons and dance lessons and swimming lessons. I helped the girls make homemade Christmas cards and Christmas cakes, and homemade biscuits and sweets to give to the teachers at Christmas. I organised birthday parties and attended birthday parties, I organised play dates and attended every school play, concert, and football match. I made world book costumes and cooked roasts and toad-in-the-in-hole.

I enjoyed every minute of it, and I wouldn't swap that time with my family for anything. But it wasn't truly me. Or I guess to be fair, it was only a part of me. And for me to be truly happy, ignoring large parts of my personality is not a great way to go.

It hurt a lot when my ex-husband told me I shouldn't have become a mum, that I wasn't a fit mum. And I was fucking furious when he tried to sabotage my relationship with my daughters telling them I was leaving them as much as him, and didn't really want them. He suggested I just wanted to leave so I could sleep with other people.

But that was just his pain talking, and I knew that even as he said it. But that candle of light deep inside me was burning brighter, and on some level, I just trusted my daughters and myself. Trusted that in time they would remember that I loved them. I trusted that I had taught them enough about people and the world that they would understand, in a way that their dad could not in that moment, that people are messy and complicated, and that although their dad was fabulous, maybe their mum was too. And trust that both their parents loved them, even if divorce and separation is very difficult. I fought to have the girls live with me, but they wanted to stay where they had grown up, and the challenging thing about equality is it works both ways. If I was going to fight for women's rights at work, I also had to accept that I couldn't pull the "kids need to stay with their mum after divorce card". So, they stayed with their dad. It nearly killed me to walk away. But if I had stayed, what would I be teaching them? That even strong capable women like us should just play along even if we were unhappy?

And I was unhappy. I'd picked a fabulous man to marry, he just didn't like me much, or liked me too much, he pushed me away and got jealous, I'm not sure which. He was proud of me, but well just wanted me to be less me as well. I loved him with all my heart, but I couldn't be a free woman with him.

I moved out on 4th July 2022, I felt liberated, and petrified, sad, scared and excited.

I had been with Gordon for 25 years, we had known each other since we were sixteen, but got together when I was 20. Last time I was dating I was a size 12 and mobile phones only made phone calls, the internet had barely launched and there were still only five channels on the TV. I got married in one world; I got divorced in a totally different one.

The full story of what happened next, a) it would be extremely X rated b) it is a whole book not a chapter, so I'll have to just give you a flavour here ...... And, I might just write that book one day,

Faced with a new situation, where I don't know much, and don't have much experience, I go on a deep dive of practical and academic research. I read everything I could get my hands on about sex and dating, from academic texts and research to websites and dating gurus. I wanted to understand and explore not just how I felt and what I wanted, but how did other people feel, how could I interpret behaviour, what did things mean? How did Bumble work? What were the rules, the official ones, but also the unofficial ones, what were the patterns and the rhythms in communication. But mostly, I wanted to find out who I was, and what I wanted. I'd spent so long knowing I could only do certain things and with one man, that faced with almost unlimited options, what did I actually want?

I was genuinely petrified that no man would ever fancy me ever again or want to have sex with me. I mean I'm a size 22, have no idea how to wear makeup, spent a decade just putting my hair up in a bun, and have never been able to flirt. Worse than that, my radar about who likes me has always been absolutely terrible. I take things quite literally, so unless someone actually comes up to me and says I fancy you, I don't think they do because well the signals are too complicated. And even if they do say that they fancy me I don't always believe them. They need to actually say something like "will you go out on a date" and even then, I've got no idea, so unless they actually make a move sexually, I'm completely in the dark.

So, at this point we have a 45 year old with a strong libido and open mind, who is ready to see what might happen, but has absolutely no skills or experience of interacting with men, or women like this. And I say both, because I had a sneaking suspicion that I liked women too, but hadn't really explored it.

It was like giving an excited toddler 25 quid and pushing them into a sweet shop. Let's face it, it was always going to be a farce. But so be it, the only way to get through this was by going through, and well, what fun it has been.

The first person I - the language just isn't there, dated isn't quite it... words that infer sexual congress like "slept with" just don't seem right. Hmmm what word to use... maybe I need to make one up? Does it matter whether the word differentiates between a connection, commitment and sex? Because that is what the language forces us to do. If I say friend, well we know what that is. Friend with benefits has come to mean something quite harsh, that doesn't sound like friendship to me. It sounds like a hook up with no commitment, but also no feelings. Dating sounds too formal and old fashioned, and whilst people do it, most people would now say that it doesn't happen straight away. Hooking up sounds transactional.

So, what is the word to use when two people meet, and there might be something, and then there is a spark, a connection? That delicious feeling that maybe two people want to get closer, physically, mentally, emotionally. But neither are quite sure what they want, or where this goes, or what the other person wants? Do they fancy me? Do I fancy them? Do we have anything in common? What do they want? Do they want a situation-ship (I hate that word too). There is a lot in some Facebook groups for women about pretty much requiring men to declare their choice of a woman from the very first moment that they interact. But that doesn't seem fair. How are the poor blokes supposed to know if someone is "the one" from date one? I'm not even sure I believe in the notion of "the one" but even if you do, how are you supposed to know who they are? You don't know someone, at that point you just have an idea of who you think they are, and they just have an idea of who they think you are. Both might be wholly inaccurate. Mmm, I'm not sure it will work for everyone, but I think I'm going to call it hypothesis testing adventures or HTA for short. That will do for now...

My first HTA was with someone I kind of knew. I liked him a lot, he was charming and intelligent and we had a mutual business client that required us to occasionally do some work together. I had absolutely no idea whether he was interested in me, and by now you've worked out that unless I asked him outright (which is largely inappropriate in almost all situations but probably especially so with someone I'm working professionally with) I've got no idea whether he likes me. So basically, I'm going in completely blind, with no skills, and no idea what I'm doing. Crazy, but actually kinda fun. Have I told you I like rollercoasters?

Again, one of the weird things about modern life is women can make the first move these days, so I don't necessarily wait to be asked, especially if the context is work related. So, I sent him an email saying it would be good to understand the client a bit better, did he fancy coffee, or lunch or something? He said it might be easier to meet for dinner, and we had a lovely evening, in which he very specifically told me that this wasn't a date. OK, boundaries set, I understand.

It was only much later it occurred to me that it was a bit odd he said it wasn't a date. I mean that is a really odd thing to say at a business meeting, and well, it meant that he had thought I thought it might be. But at the time, I just took it literally.

I didn't see him for a few months, and then we ended up catching up about work again, only this time we went to a lovely wine bar and had some food. Now it isn't odd to have business meetings over a glass or two of wine, and to end up chatting about all sorts of things other than work. I remember in my early days as a senior manager I thought that I was somehow cheating if I talked about anything social with work colleagues. But I realised that actually that way I was just generally seen as a scary bitch, and that small talk has a social purpose. So, I started to learn to chat at work. Which I love, I love chatting to people, and am insatiably curious about people, I love to hear about what they care about, and how they are, I enjoy listening to people talk about their families. And I guess that is why I became a Samaritan; I figured I might as well put my enjoyment to good use if I could. Because I'm not sure everyone else is as interested.

I remember watching a clip of someone saying to someone "god how long do I have to pretend to be interested in them". Sorry what? People are pretending to be interested? For what purpose? Why would they pretend? What you mean they aren't actually interested? Why on earth not? Every single person is like the most interesting and complex puzzle of experience in the world.

You can hear the penny drop. I really do find everyone that interesting, I love hearing about the details of their job or their lives, because I'm insatiably curious. I'm not pretending, I don't really do pretending. If anyone ever saw some of my attempts at amateur dramatics in my teens, they will know, I can't act for toffee. I'm no good at pretending.

Realising that small talk actually makes working with people better, and as I absolutely love it, I was like, well then win win.

This seems to work even more in business, where building rapport with customers and clients is vital, and it is more acceptable to go for a working lunch or drink than it is in the public sector. So back to that wine bar.

He was sitting opposite me, and I was learning a lot about our shared client (all useful stuff, makes my job much easier, much of what I do requires understanding the people, their motivations, their history, their why, and this shit was gold dust to me). And well I know nothing about wine, but I love learning about new things, so I was asking lots of questions, he clearly knew a lot about wine, and I think he liked that I was asking questions. He asked a bit about my family and I explained I was in the process of getting divorced, and I kind of explained that I was exploring the idea of being poly.

So how does a newly free woman explain that quite frankly she has no desire to immediately lose herself in another monogamous relationship but doesn't want to be celibate? I knew I didn't just want casual sex either; I like the emotional connection. If you saw who I'm attracted to you'd struggle to find a physical type, gender, or occupation. But there is a pattern. I like people who are interested in different things to me, I like people who have a heart of gold, but are struggling in some way, I like people who have interesting minds (Side note that this isn't strictly intelligence, I'm definitely a fan of Howard Gardners Multiple Intelligences Theory - I think we are too narrow in our definitions, I see intellectual sparks in creatives, and sportsmen, people who wouldn't necessarily see themselves as intelligent, but I do).

I'm delaying a bit, stringing the story out, because well the next bit is both wonderful and incredibly painful. There is a reason that the best advice suggests a period of abstinence for at least a year or two after a divorce, but my desire for connection was too great. I don't regret what happened next, it was probably for me the only way through. When something difficult needs to be done, I'm a let's dive in headfirst kind of gal, not a let's slowly tiptoe towards it.

In my mind, we were just having a very abstract conversation about being divorced and polyamory as a life choice, and it was mostly just me talking at this point. Then it came time to walk back to the station to get my train. I was slightly tipsy by this point, and well I'd had a lovely afternoon. I knew I liked the guy, but I had assumed that it was one-sided and that it was just going to be a very pleasant business relationship, and I was totally OK with that. We got to the train station and paused, and shit that is one of those uncomfortable moments. Do you shake hands? Do nothing? Hug? I was still busy thinking what exactly was the correct social ending to this kind of thing when he completely took me by surprise...

And kissed me...

Huh?

I pulled away somewhat surprised, but rather pleasantly... I didn't move away, and he kissed me again. Mmm, this was nice, I reached up with my hand and started stroking the back of his neck and he put his hand on my waist and then moved it up to my boob... WTF?

OK, time to go, I needed to get that train... and I was gone. I didn't really understand what was going on and I needed time to process.

He invited me out for drinks and dinner the next weekend. And he really pulled out the stops, I'm not that easy to impress, but he was a total gentlemen; the basement gin bar was romantic and classy and the French restaurant chic but relaxed. I had a hotel booked as I was in town for a few days, but he invited me back to his place.

The first time I had sex after my ex could have gone horrifically wrong. But again, a fluke of my personality saved me. When I'm enjoying myself I kind of lose myself in the moment, and well I really do like sex, so I just forgot all of my inhibitions and was really enjoying myself. But then it all got too much.

I mean the only time I'd had three orgasms in an evening prior to that night, had involved an Idris Elba binge and a rabbit, so the reality of a man wanting and being able to get me to that point in real life was somewhat overwhelming. Whilst vaguely being rather pleased that he was making so much effort to please, when I thought he might try to help me get to four my head was literally exploding with pleasure and I wasn't actually sure I could cope so I asked him to stop. Slightly bemused about my desire to stop having pleasure, he looked at me quizzically, and I was just honest, and before I realised that it probably wasn't a good idea I said...

"It's all a bit much, I've not been naked with anyone other than my ex-husband for 25 years".

Whoops, probably not a great idea to mention your ex-husband actually during sex, and well I'd opened up a level of vulnerability that I really hadn't meant to and what happened next could have very much destroyed me if it had gone differently.

I mean in hindsight I already felt damn lucky that he had wanted me to take my clothes off at all, and seemed genuinely attracted to me, the skill and desire to please was simply a little too much, and well he could have crushed my emerging hope that well perhaps actually my life might actually include not just sex but great sex.

But in fact he did one of the kindest things anyone has ever done, ever, for which I will be truly grateful, forever, he simply reached out (I had moved away and turned round suddenly incredibly vulnerable). He gently placed his hand in on my back and said

"Oh Aime..." with such kindness I almost cried.

He then just gave me a massive hug, and in that moment, I suddenly realised, it might just all be OK.

Rebound relationships are usually a car crash, and our brief sojourn was never meant to be forever. But it was lovely to be wined and dined for a few months and taken to romantic restaurants, to talk for hours and hours and then enjoy each other's bodies. Never in the past being one to say what I actually wanted, or say when I was upset (good girls don't complain), he also got the full force of a toddler trying to learn to explain her feelings (me learning to be a free woman). I shouted at him when he upset me, and sent angry WhatsApp messages, and I think I blocked him three times in as many months. But each time he dealt with my emotions kindly and in an understanding way, apologising and letting me talk myself down. In the end I managed to get to a point where I could talk myself back into a calm space without even blocking him. Quite a learning curve!

In hindsight I wasn't ready for a relationship, and he didn't want one, but I fall in love easily so it was still hard when he let me down we had a massive fight and suddenly it was all over.

Life was already difficult enough, and to get through difficult things we all need positive things. So, it was especially hard, especially as I didn't really understand. Had I done something wrong, was I not good enough?

It would have been easy of me to have been destroyed or broken beyond repair at this point. To turn yet another rejection into self-blame.

But I'm an eternal optimist. I could write this brief affair off as a disaster, I could get angry with him for targeting a woman clearly vulnerable. But I'm going to take the more adult approach. It was two people both seeking to find connection in a lonely world. Neither of us wanted a traditional relationship, and well I was probably just a bit "too much" for him. I can be overwhelming, intense. But that is OK. It is who I am. I occasionally bump into him, we still after all have a client in common, and I'd be lying if I said I didn't still have feelings for him, but we have found a bumpy friendship. We are both very capable of being professional and I doubt anyone that knows us would ever know our secret. But I kind of like that. If I'm angry, it is more that I'm angry we couldn't find a way to keep enjoying each other's company. I had very much decided that polyamory was my route forward, so I didn't have problem with him having other lovers, but it needed to be ethical. There is a great book called the "Ethical Slut" by Janet W. Hardy and Dossie Easton and I've read it cover to cover.

Men have an interesting reaction to me saying that I am poly. Most tend to see it just as a green light for sex, or an excuse to cheat on their wives. It is neither. It is about recognising that at this point in my life, I don't know exactly what I want, and I am accepting of myself, but I am a lot. And that actually an adult way to deal with that for now is to spread around the intensity. But to do so in an honest way... I have some rules.

1. Everyone in the relationship has to be consenting (that means no partners that don't realise they are in a polyamorous relationship).
2. I'm not interested in living with anyone, merging my life or finances, or introducing them to my family (much to my Dad's dismay who really wants to meet some of the interesting people I've been spending my time with - but if I can be too much on my own, me plus the whole Millward clan is a complete and utter overwhelm, just ask the three lovely people who married in!).
3. I don't need or want texts every day, and am quite happy with going weeks or even months with no contact, as long

as I feel there is respect and I know what is going on.

4. I do want emotional connection. And it tends to be very intense... if that isn't your bag, that is OK ...... but I don't do hook ups just for the sake of it... for me sex is something more than that.

5. Condoms - seriously guys, I know you like it better without, but let's be adult about this, and I'm just as worried about giving you something as you giving me something.

Realising that perhaps I did actually have the potential to still have relationships and be attractive I decided to try internet dating.

Bumble seemed to be a friendly and female led option. So, I created my profile. I knew my slight confidence about my desirability was fledgling and fragile at best, so it was a bold move. But with most of my social circle being married, it was realistically the only option. I was terrified. I set myself a KPI to try and manage my expectations. If I got twelve likes in a week then that would be a success I decided. I launched my profile and then turned my phone off and went to bed. I couldn't bear to find out whether I would be ignored and undesired for the rest of my life.

I opened my phone with incredible trepidation the morning after, hoping for just one like, please just one like to prove to myself that it was possible, that I could do this Internet dating thing...

And I looked in shock, 439 likes, since the night before. Holy fuck!

And with those two experiences (my rebound HTA and my dive into internet dating) I knew it was going to be OK. A chatty person by nature I enjoyed all the Bumble and WhatsApp interactions, and the videos and HTAs that followed. I leaned into learning and playing and exploring my own sexuality. I was now free to do anything and everything I wanted and the potential was fabulous. Highlights include the first time I kissed a woman, my HTA with someone famous, the old flames that suddenly reappeared, an online sex party and a secret event where I had to climb through a mirror to a secret bar and I won a pair of long black latex gloves...

But well, that is another book entirely...

The point for now is that in my broken and bruised state, the interactions and desire and kindness from the lovers I came across helped soothe my pain and rebuild my confidence. Whilst not every connection worked out (I was so prolific chatting to people on Bumble that they started incentivising me by giving a donation to charity each time I started a new chat) I was gradually learning how to be a free woman.

The idea of work/life balance is farcical. It is all just life. We are individuals, workers, lovers, businesspeople, friends, daughters, and it all just gets mixed up. When things are going badly at work it has an impact on the rest of our lives, and when things are difficult in our personal lives it impacts on our ability to do great work and be creative. So, my divorce and adapting to post-divorce life, is as much a part of this story as the rest of it.

A special thank you to Gavin, who has the amazing ability to always make me feel wonderful, and unlike my other polys actually wanted to be named in this book! He is a fabulous HTA and whilst I've got loads of amazing love letters written by others, and I've had poetry and even a play written in my name, he did offer to write a song on his next album about me and call it Leek Princess if I named him in this book. So, Gavin, you are here, thank you for being there for me and always making me feel amazing, and I look forward to seeing Leek Princess on Spotify sometime next year... (I'm not sure he actually thought I'd go through with naming him... so this should be interesting!)

But seriously, thank you to all those lovers who made me feel better, and eased me back into this new world. I'm not exactly sure what I want next, but the initial intoxication has finally calmed a little, and I can explore at a more sedate and healthy pace. But I am no longer worried that I will ever be without intimate connections. Because actually, in a world where almost everyone is lonely, all I ever have to do is connect (oh and the boobs help, apparently men and women like boobs - who knew!).

Chapter 11

Getting back on the horse: Dinner with Royalty and driving sheep over London Bridge

They say that if you fall off a horse, you need to get back on it soon. I guess the logic is that after you've had a fall and hurt yourself and are probably a little bit scared, you need to face that fear and get back into the saddle. And do it quickly. Because if you don't you might never get back in the saddle ever again. I don't know how true it is, but I guess I believed it. So faced with being told by a group of old white very conservative men that I was useless and untrustworthy what better than to find an even scarier bunch and see if I could cope.

Life seems to have a funny way of throwing me the things that I need. Not necessarily the things I want mind. Winning the lottery and meeting Idris Elba and him falling madly in love with me, being high on the list of things I'd like. But I guess perhaps the truth is that there are plenty of opportunities in life to find the things we need if we are just open to them. And if you are a chatty, friendly type like me, then the opportunities are almost endless.

My Coopers' journey started as if it were a carefully plotted and scripted film on location. It was twilight on a beautiful sunny and warm early autumn evening. I was standing overlooking the Thames at a private champagne reception after hours in the Tower of London. The sun was setting, it was that golden hour the photographers love so much. There were around 30 of us, I had been invited by an old friend who was a Liveryman of the Worshipful Company of Coopers. I had been a School Captain at the Coopers Company and Coborn School, a state school founded and run by the Worshipful Company, but at that point I didn't really know much more about London Livery Companies or the Worshipful Company, except that they had been the old white men in gowns and furs with medals and chains that handed out whatever school prize I'd won that year at prize giving. But I kinda knew my friend Sarah was something big in the Company and that she had some sort of role. To be honest she had me, at "Aime do you fancy coming to the Tower of London for some drinks with some interesting people". I mean who wouldn't?

So I was standing there and we met the Deputy Governor of the Tower, a lovely woman who dropped by to say hello on her way to dinner and the Company Mascot, a beautiful shire horse was there hot foot from meeting the Duke and Duchess of Cambridge (gets around that horse, better connected than any of us!). I didn't really know anyone, except Sarah and her lovely husband and fabulous daughters, but it was a fabulous evening, and well a night with the Coopers is always a night for the sharing of amazing conversations, I mean most of those people I can't admit to ever knowing, and the stories they tell should never be shared!

So, as the light disappeared below the horizon, we were escorted into the Tower proper, and invited into the Keys. The Keys is probably one of the most fortified and exclusive private members clubs in London. I hadn't actually been in the Tower of London before, so I was quite surprised that as well as being a palace, a castle, and a live military base, it is also a tourist attraction and a village. Quite a mixture, you can perhaps understand why I feel connected. I like complicated. Inside the walls the families of the Yeoman Guards (otherwise known as Beefeaters) live, and the Keys is their local pub. They run it themselves and you can only go in with an invite from one of them. It is literally a place you cannot buy your way into, a rare thing in today's world. The Coopers have a long and warm connection with the Tower, the military generally, the Governors of the Tower and the Beefeaters. Traditionally the Coopers Beadle (a part time role to run our events - think master of ceremonies) is a Beefeater. Did you know there have been more people in space than have ever been Beefeater's?

The Keys itself is actually a warm and welcoming place more like a friendly local pub than a posh private members' club, it just has slightly more historic memorabilia and stories. There is something really quite cool about being served Beefeater gin and tonic in the Keys, when the rest of the public have been asked to leave, by a real life Beefeater. We were then asked to join the amazing Ceremony of the Keys, the ceremonial locking of the Tower that has happened every evening for hundreds of years, and is completed in complete silence and has never been recorded... and we also got a tour, spooky and somewhat eerie to hear stories of beheadings, murder and torture in the dark in an empty fortress, when everyone else had gone home...

I was really quite glad to get back to the Keys and have a few more drinks after our spooky tour. After probably three glasses of champagne and well, plenty of gins and tonics, the Master of the Worshipful Company of Coopers came and sat down opposite me in the Keys. It is a role held for a year, it is a great honour, and comes with all sorts of special privileges and opportunities. I had never met the Master before, but the Master that year was a rather fabulous Scot who I knew had been an Engineer and had built bridges and things. So already quite overwhelmed with the whole location and well probably a few too many drinks he said...

"So Aime, I hear you do HR, we have never really had any and I wondered what your thoughts are about how we might introduce it".

Oh fuck... I was going to have to pitch about HR, to an organisation that has existed for more than 800 years, is steeped in tradition, has never had HR, despite having staff, and I'm drunk... excellent...

I'm not exactly sure what I said next, I think it had something to do with renovating listed buildings and wanting to put in electricity and toilets without destroying the fabric of the building, and something about design needing to be simple and that whilst the Americans had spent millions inventing a pen where the ink could flow in space the Russians had taken a pencil - to be honest I've no idea what I said.

But it can't have been that bad, because I ended up being asked to introduce the first HR and policies into this veneered ancient institution, and to be an inaugural part of the first Employee and Remuneration Committee.

I was scared stiff. The board of the company (historically called the court) is full of the cream of the British establishment. There are captains of industry, ex-Lord Mayors of London, numerous Judges, lawyers and some incredibly senior people in the British military. The amount of money moving through the room is something rather intimidating.

But then something entirely unexpected and rather wonderful happened. It turned out that being a bright bolshy, opinionated and confident woman who wasn't scared to challenge them and argue with them, and who enjoyed to drink and talk and eat and tell stories, fit right in.

But of course, I didn't know that right away. Getting the gig is one thing. Pulling it off, is something else entirely...

So, I set about helping the Worshipful Company of Coopers get their payroll and HR processes and policies and procedures up to scratch. Within a year, it was all up to code, and fit for purpose. Not bad considering I had to do everything via committee, and at the first committee one person said "well we haven't had HR for 800 years, why do we need it now?". It wasn't easy, there was a lot of debate, but most of it was about trying to explain why things needed doing. It helped that I did two lots of recruitment for them, both of which should have been impossible appointments, both of which went meticulously well and offered the Platinum standard of headhunting, I did all the work myself, and suggested one candidate each time (both of which they appointed and have loved!).

Before joining the Coopers, I didn't really know anything about the military. But I've been learning, and have had some amazing behind the scenes tours, all of which I'm not allowed to share, but let's just say it was kind of exciting to see on the News that the new Minister of Defence had done the same thing I had done with the Coopers a few weeks before! Oh, and they let me press buttons, I like pressing buttons.... If you look carefully on the walls at Coopers Hall you might find my smiling face on an RAF plane in a framed photograph...

One of our connections is HMS President. I got all excited because I thought this was a ship. But then I found out that every Navy base and Ship is given an HMS title (didn't look at all silly when I asked that question 😊). HMS President[42] is the only London based Navy Base, it is the HQ of the Royal Navy Reserves and is just next to Tower Bridge. It has one of the coolest balconies, which numerous films have used as locations, and is considered the spiritual base of 007 as Ian Fleming was based there. So, when I got an invite to join dinner after a Court meeting that was being held there, I was like, hell yes!

I turned up and enjoyed champagne overlooking Tower Bridge and then had a lovely dinner. After dinner we had what was called the Stirrup Cup.[43] Now I thought this would actually be a cup of some sort, but no, it is military code for basically where the host chooses to allow you to stay for one more drink before the road. The host for that night was a great bloke, and although we were all due to be chucked out, he got out the good stuff and asked us to stay. Another lock in, excellent! A few of us stayed to carry on drinking. It was a lovely night, amazing company, and a fabulous location, just made better when the drinking games started...

First of all I was asked would I do "danger port". Well quite frankly it depends on what danger we are talking about...

They took me to a wooden box on the wall. It was a container with apparently an expensive bottle of port within it. The idea was would you drink a shot.

Well I'm not a big fan of port but...

Ahh but that is not the danger. You see the person who draws an empty glass must pay for the next bottle.

Ahh, OK so I might get a free shot of port, or an empty glass and a hefty bill... now I see the risk. How much is an expensive bottle of port I wondered, maybe about £250? Most of the people around me said no to the danger port, but unfettered I said I'd give it a go. Then I tried to open the case to see how much port there was inside. The wooden case opened, but the bottle was inside a beautiful velvet bag, there was a note attached...

"Nice try..."

Ahh, possibly not the first person to try that.

OK so well I was just going to have to do it. Spurred on by a crowd, at this point I took my shot, and there was a cheer as I got my port, and I downed it.

Geed on by the crowd and the alcohol and the playful feeling in the room, I asked what other drinking games there were. The Commander of HMS President walked over to the fireplace, well there is this...

I looked down, it appeared to be an empty shell casing that had exploded, about two foot tall with a jagged edge.

"It's heavy Aime, don't...

Too late I'd already picked it up - I'm stronger than I look.

"Well, what's the game then?"

Well, you put it on the floor.

I put it on the floor.

You stand next to it with a partner back-to-back and lock your arms over the shell, then wrestle till one of you gives in.

Hmmm properly dangerous then... falling on that could be nasty, the edges were sharp...

But I was drunk and in good spirits then, forget the fact we were all dressed in black tie and I had a dress on...

"Who's going to do this with me then?"

I made eye contact with one of the past masters, and suggested he might. He looked at me in shock and said...

"I'm not fighting a girl"

There was a stunned silence (everyone was watching us at this point).

How was Aime going to react to being called a girl, and the suggestion that she couldn't fight (I was school fencing captain, and in one interesting competition we had made the Eton boys cry because they were upset about being beaten by a bunch of Essex girls) and well I'm not exactly a slim slip of a lass.

But this isn't about destroying anyone. This is about finding a way through the mire of changing social norms and being kind to each other.

I laughed and grabbed his arm, and picked up the shell casing.

"Well as he's too scared to take me on, then I'm claiming a victory".

Someone snapped a picture, and the room burst into laughter and smiles, a difficult moment passed.

When I woke up the next morning, someone had sent me the picture...

Oh crap...

That was like a really senior member of the company...

I texted his wife (I'd have texted him, but I didn't have his number).

"OK so like how much trouble am I in?" I asked.

She sent lots of smiling emojis and said

"You're OK Aime, he thought it was hilarious, we all did".

Phew...

As hazing goes, it wasn't that bad, but I had won some credibility, not easily gained in those sorts of environments. I was becoming one of them.

A month or so later, I saw him and most of the senior members of the company (nearly all male). It was the Cloker Service, a historic event where everyone turns up in their full gowns and we get some really interesting guest vicars. Afterwards there is dinner, and unusually it doesn't have a seating plan.

I didn't know where to sit, so I just sat down, and five very interesting men sat around me. The ex-Master I had declared the win from sat next to me, opposite him was an ex-Lord Mayor of London, and next to him a high-level banker, and then next to him the most senior criminal Judge (retired) and also a senior educator. They had all chosen to sit next to me, and the conversation was lively and amazing. At one point I asked a pointed question about the nature of the judicial system, and sitting next to me the Past

Master interrupted me...

"Give the guy a chance to actually answer Aime" he said with a huge smile...

I had to have my sister tell me about banter, but she explained that whilst some people are offended (and rightly so) by some male dominated cultures, when they start to make jokes about you, and make banter, it is actually because you have been accepted as one of them...

And that night, I very much felt like I had been accepted.

It was all going well. Whilst there was part of me that was kind of waiting for it to all get horrible (there was still some trauma left from being at ENC) I held my nerve, and they didn't seem to hate me. In fact, I was invited to the next level of status in the Company, full Livery, only two years after being awarded Freeman Status (which is kind of like probation), I was kind of surprised. It had happened very quickly, and it was for life. It also included being nominated to be given the Freedom of the City of London, a wonderfully traditional ceremony that is only awarded by invitation at the Guildhall. I can now do all sorts of things including vote for the Lord Mayor of London and herd sheep across London Bridge. And, while it slightly amuses me that I was made a Freeman not a Freewoman, I like the fact that I have officially been recognised as a Free person, in the city of London at least!

When I turned up at Common Hall to receive my official Livery status, which includes a ceremony where you are literally given a robe, I didn't really believe they were actually going to give it to me. I mean how the hell had a young, rebellious, left leaning bleeding heart like me been given Livery status? Although I knew that the votes had already been cast and I was already in, I was suddenly incredibly nervous as I waited in the anti-room.

Now at this point I should probably talk a little about clothes. Clothes are very powerful, and for a woman especially they say a lot. My friend Katy has taught me a lot about the politics of clothes, and especially seditious pockets[45]. Coopers events have four dress codes

1. White tie - very posh, reserved mainly only for royal events and events at Mansion House. Men wear tails, women should wear gloves.
2. Black tie - a more relaxed version of white tie that you have probably all heard of.
3. Business smart - the men wear suits and ties.
4. Smart casual - still fairly smart, jackets required, but no suit is needed.

Both White tie and Black Tie can be switched for full military dress (which is a whole different level of complicated!).

I'm not sure whether it is easier or harder to be a man as opposed to a woman at these kinds of events. Being a man makes it very clear what you should wear, but also doesn't give you much room for individuality. But as a woman, the rules are much more fluid. This gives more potential for individuality, but also means that you can get it totally wrong. Common Hall is Business Smart. One option is to try to dress like a man. For example wearing a business suit. But a suit jacket and tight short skirt makes me look absolutely terrible. I am a woman of ample curves, and whilst those styles look AMAZING on many women, they make me look and feel like a frumpy ugly wannabe. I usually get round this by wearing dresses and skirts, often in bright colours. But what the hell was I going to wear to be made a Liveryman?

I didn't want to be too rebellious, so I wore a black shirt dress that looked quite smart. But it felt like a bit too much of a watering down of who I am, so I paired it with a pair of rainbow coloured fishnet tights and black patent DMs. I felt that I had made the right choice for me, adapting a little, but trying to hold on to who I am too. After all I don't want them to accept me, if the only way I'm going to be accepted is to change who I am. But I still wanted to be accepted, and I didn't want to go too far.

I was nervous, really nervous. But the event went well, and when I had to stand up and say something in front of everyone it went OK. I sat down, and the person next to me said I did well. It was a BBC TV presenter, so I'll take that.

Then I got drunk.

I don't think people realise that I get nervous.

Of course, I do! I just do things anyway.

That day I was really nervous, but well they didn't have to let me in, and I was so happy. I had managed to get back on the horse and not fall flat on my face.

Then, shortly after becoming a Liveryman something happened that simply warmed my heart.

The Coopers were invited to a very posh do by the Worshipful Company of Drapers.[46] Even within the Livery Companies there are hierarchies, and the Drapers are considered to be one of the Great Twelve. Kings and Queens have been members, and Queen Elizabeth II and King Charles III were/are both members. The Drapers are incredibly wealthy, and their hall is like a palace. They were holding a special event to thank the Household division's[47] involvement in the late Queen's funeral. It was invite only, and the costs were covered by the Drapers. The Coopers are also affiliated to the Household division, so along with a few other Company's we were given a handful of tickets. The Master and Clerk could give these tickets to whomever they wished. As thank you's and as gifts, but also with the recognition that guests would be ambassadors for the company. There were no plus ones's, the only way you got into the room is because you were personally invited.

The Master and Clerk knew that I would absolutely love an event like this. So, to say thank you for all the work I had done, they invited me along.

It was already going to be posh enough, but we got a last minute hushed piece of information, it was going to be hosted by the Princess Royal, Princess Anne, my favourite Royal (I mean the others are warming on me, but she is the quietest most hardworking of the Royals and I think she is just wonderful).

It was an absolutely glorious summer evening, just me and about 200 men, mostly in uniform. There were very few women, and of those most didn't wear a long black ballgown.

As I wandered round the champagne reception, I knew very few people, and I was feeling giddy with excitement (this was like Cinderella going to the ball, only I was wearing comfy knickers under my posh ball gown and comfy shoes - cuz no-one looks at my feet, and I wasn't aiming to get a man, just be myself). Walking into one room, each group of men that I walked up to kind of shunned me. I walked on, I wasn't welcome. I kept going till a group of four military men allowed me to join. All very senior officers we actually had an interesting conversation about HR (because actually managing staff is a big part of being a senior officer in the military). As we were called to dinner, I walked away, then went back and said thank you to the most senior man who had made it clear I was welcome. I thanked him for including me. He apologised for the fact that some of his colleagues had ignored me, there was still lots to change he said. Then he said something very kind. He had apparently been talking to the Ambassador to Washington a few months ago, and she had also said that when she walked into rooms like this, she was also often shunned. But he smiled, and said

"But she told me that there was a strategy, and Aime, without realising it, you just did everything a senior diplomat would do".

I grinned. He had made me feel that although I may not always be welcomed by everyone in rooms like this, I had some skills. And well he said I was like an Ambassador. Shit, I was taking that.

Dinner[48] was amazing, you will struggle to find me amongst the red military uniforms but I'm there...

After dinner, well then it was drinks outside. It was a warm summer evening, and I had the most amazing conversations. The Coopers Clerk caught up with me and said

"Aime there is someone who I think you'd like to talk to... come with me".

Good bloke our Clerk, and he introduced me to Vern[49] Vern and I talked for ages, and what stories he had to tell!!!

I left in the early hours of the morning, and as I was waiting for my Uber feeling as happy as Larry someone came up to me and said

"You look amazing!"

I'll take that, I'll take it all.

I think as far as falling off your horse, and then daring to get back on, I didn't do too badly.

Ahh I've forgotten the sheep!

Well, as I was told that I could herd sheep across London Bridge, one clear Sunday morning, along with a number of other Freeman I did just that!

I'm not entirely sure what the Coopers think of me, quite frankly I don't have the guts to ask. But generally, they seem to like and respect me. At a time when I was feeling very low, they made me feel useful and capable again. And for that I will always be truly grateful.

PART FOUR:
What I did next

Chapter 12
The HR and Workers Trade Union

The first silk mill in Staffordshire was built in 1755 in Congleton, only a few miles from where I live now, one of the first mechanised factories at the beginning of the industrial revolution. I can date my family back to the area I now live in Leek, Staffordshire for more than 300 years (the last person to be hanged for murder in Leek was my great great great grandfather!). We were miller's or mylen-weard (old English for keeper of the mill) even before my family began working in the silk and dye works of Leek. My maiden name is Millward.

Someone once said to me that although I was thoroughly middle class on the outside, if you cut me in half, I am working class. And there is some truth to that. I am the first woman of any of my ancestors to ever get a degree. My grandmother, despite getting into the grammar school, was not allowed to go. Instead, she left school at fourteen and went to work in the mills of Leek to help support her six younger brothers and sisters and the family. And when he got back from being a prisoner of the second world war, my grandfather worked in the Leek dye works. Neither finished school or got a single qualification, although he did win many awards for Ballroom Dancing.

I had been a member of a big national trade union when things started going wrong at ENC. But, it is really hard to get help from a Trade Union when the local rep is making allegations. I did get some excellent support for some of the time from a regional rep, but the Trade Union as a whole was stuck in some very old fashioned ways of thinking. When I found myself without a job and a career, it occurred to me that I might make a good Trade Union rep, so I applied for a full-time job. I didn't get shortlisted, not enough specific Trade Union experience apparently.

Then a really good friend came to me, she was being treated terribly by her employer, and wondered if I could help as an HR professional. I looked into it and found that whilst it was perfectly possible to offer advice to any company in the role of HR practitioner without any qualifications or accreditation, I wasn't allowed to charge to advise an individual. It is all because the government class this as giving financial advice therefore it is covered by the FCA (Financial Conduct Authority). The logic is that if I provided advice to someone where it could lead to a financial settlement, I needed to be registered by the FCA. I asked around the HR community, and also did some research. Whilst it was clear that I would need to be registered, it wasn't clear how I could get registered, and it would probably take thousands of pounds and about a year. When I asked around, only one person appeared to have got through this process, and this was years ago under another regime, it seemed like a dead end.

Then I had an idea.

A crazy idea.

Well, I thought, if I can't join a Trade Union, could I create a Trade Union? There are plenty of rules and protections about how a Trade Union can operate, but how about creating one?

Again, I did some research.

There have been trade associations across the world for thousands of years. In the UK guilds evolved into the London Livery Companies, and Trade Unions. Anti-establishment by nature, Trade Unions were originally illegal in the UK. They were legalised in 1872 after a Royal Commission on Trade Unions in 1867 agreed that their establishment was to the advantage of both employers and employees.

The Trade Union and Labour Relations (Consolidation) Act 1992 sets out the legal definition of "Trade Union" in section 1.

"In this Act a "Trade Union" means an organisation (whether temporary or permanent) which consists wholly or mainly of workers of one or more descriptions and whose principal purposes include the regulation of relations between workers of that description or those descriptions and employers or employer's associations".

Temporary?

If a Trade Union could be temporary, that suggested to me that it didn't need necessarily to be too complicated, or big or overly bureaucratic surely?

And well, it sounded like a Trade Union was a Trade Union if it acted like a Trade Union.

The 1992 Act also talks about a Certification Process and a Certification Officer who is a Civil Servant. I read all the information, and rang their office. There was a process to ask the Certification Officer to confirm whether a Trade Union was a Trade Union or not. But what I wanted to find out, was did I have to get permission? Looking through the court records (when I research I deep dive! Blame the law degree and an insatiably curious mind) and the Certification Officer, a government appointment, had been turning down every prospective Trade Union that applied. Strange that, the Conservative government have never exactly been pro Trade Union.

I knew that I couldn't run a Trade Union with the traditional business model. That works by getting lots of people to pay a small membership each month, then volunteers help those members that need it, and the membership fee pays for head office and legal support for members. It is only possible to pay for enough support if you get thousands of members. So that wasn't going to work.

But pretty much every other industry has disruptors, people who are doing things differently, creating different business models. Why not Trade Unions? The world of work has changed almost unrecognisably in the last hundred years, so why shouldn't Trade Unions?

In some ways, a traditional Trade Union is a collaborative group, but it also kind of operates like an insurance policy. So why couldn't we have a pay as you go Trade Union I wondered?

I rang the Certification Officer's team to talk through what I was proposing. They were not impressed; they clearly didn't think I should be able to do that. But I was still trying to find out, whether they could stop me...

Eventually as she got more frustrated, I just asked (politely mind) whether she could stop me. She got flustered and said that there were rules to follow if I was a Trade Union, and if I operated one then I would have to follow those. I said I was happy to follow the rules but was it true that she could only reject me if I actually applied, that if I didn't apply then she only had any authority if she deemed me to be a Trade Union. The irony was that she only had power over us if we were a Trade Union. Or asked her if we were one.

So, my intention was just to be one, and not ask permission.

There is a point in anyone's journey from good girl to free woman when you stop asking "Am I allowed?" And start asking, "Can they stop me?".

The Certification Officer said

"If you operate as a Trade Union I will find out and you will have to follow the rules".

I said

"Excellent, I hope that in a few years time you will contact me, tell me I am a Trade Union and tell me I have to follow the rules, I will be over the moon. But until then, I take it that you can't tell me I can't be a Trade Union in this way".

Exasperated, she slammed the phone down on me. Rather unusual and undignified for a Civil Servant.

I smiled.

I'll take that as a yes then. To become a Trade Union, well I just have to put my big girl pants on and be one, I thought.

So, on the 2nd December 2019 I sat at my desk in Leicestershire and decided that I would will the HR and Workers Trade Union into existence. And because I decided it was, it was.

Magic...

Well not quite.

Now I needed to see whether I could actually pull this off. I mean I was only really a Trade Union if I could persuade other people that I was a Trade Union.

So I went back to that friend, we went to the pub, and she asked me again if I could help.

"Well" I said, "I have just set up a Trade Union. You could be my first member, and I could be your rep and help you through this."

All the bullying had been too much for my friend and she was off sick with stress. They had written lots of formal letters to her and were inviting her into a capability hearing to consider her absence. She also wanted to know if she could complain about the treatment she was receiving.

I knew her personal circumstances, and that the job was well below her skill set, and that financially she could survive without her income (risk management is a real thing, if she had been a single mum with no other source of income, then another strategy might have been more useful). But I asked her what she wanted.

She said she never wanted to go back there, she wanted to complain, and she wanted to find herself again and find out what she could do.

"Then don't go to the meeting" I said.

She looked at me quizzically, as the penny slowly dropped.

"Just don't go. I'll contact them on your behalf and say that you don't want to go, and that we need to rearrange".

She'd been so badly treated, and was feeling so low, it hadn't occurred to her that she didn't have to accept what they said.

"But surely I'll get in trouble".

"Well eventually, they will seek to dismiss you, but you don't want to stay anyway, and I can negotiate and support you through your exit. It's not like they can force you to attend, they can't send the police to drag you in!"

A slight smile spread across my friend's face as she realised there was another way.

One of the things I do as a Trade Union Rep is show members that there are other ways of looking at the world. Other solutions to the problems they face. Push me or someone I care about in a corner, and I get creative. And that is what I do as a Trade Union rep. It's why I'm called The Employment Genie.

You see, she was upset and felt trapped because she couldn't see that she had more power than she realised she had. She thought that she had to do what they told her to do.

Until I reminded her that she was a free woman too. Yes, of course there are consequences to making decisions (this book shows my story is hardly without consequences). But feeling you have choice is still empowering.

And at that moment, she realised she could just walk away, and that would stop them being able to hurt and upset her ever again.

She hugged me.

Sometimes all people need is a good friend to light the way down an alternative path.

All I did was remind her what was possible.

And then I supported her all the way through what happened next!

She never did go back in. I helped her negotiate a settlement agreement, and she left and set up her own business. It hasn't always been easy, and she's worked incredibly hard, but she really hasn't looked back. We caught up today on the phone, as I was thinking about writing this story, and we both realised that we were both doing the things we were always meant to be. I'm not going to tell you who she is, because I'm not sure if she wants her story told. But I can say that her business is now massive and doing amazingly well. And she is so much happier now she is a free woman! I see her posts on social media, and it makes me feel so good to see her thriving. I always knew she had it in her!

And her employer, a massive national company, accepted that the HR and Workers Trade Union existed.

I smiled quietly when it was done. It might have been a crazy idea, but we'd just had our first client, and our first win

I had actually set up a Trade Union.

The **HR and Workers Trade Union** now existed.

On meeting me, some people think I'm a little posh. It does depend on the context of where I am and what I'm wearing, but I think people would mostly consider me pretty soundly middle class (the posh veneer doesn't last long!). I know we don't talk about class anymore, but well, I think we should all talk a lot about all the things we don't talk about. All those taboos hold lots of emotional issues, and well, I think, however uncomfortable it is, talking helps (but then I am a big talker!), listening helps too though, and I didn't think I was as good at it as I could be, but running the Trade Union has helped, as has becoming a Samaritan.

And the two things are linked and help each other. As a Samaritan listening volunteer there are very strict rules, we aren't allowed to talk about ourselves, or tell the listener anything about ourselves, we can't judge or make suggestions or give advice. I don't have a problem not judging, I'm not a very judgy person. But not tell stories, not making suggestions, not giving advice? I didn't think I could do it, and I didn't think it would work.

I was wrong on both counts. There is something truly magical about holding space for a stranger in their darkest hour, and I have had had a number who are suicidal, including one who was in the process of killing herself. You have to deal with all of your emotions, notice them, recognise them, feel them (no bottling up or ignoring them) but then focus entirely on the caller's emotional needs. The desire to help is incredibly strong, the desire to comfort is incredibly strong. But by just holding space, by being kind and supportive, and listening and accepting the reality of the person who is calling, something truly magical happens. They feel heard and acknowledged, and I can feel a caller go from shouting and crying or not talking at all, to feeling a little bit better, even laughing. A strong bond is created, and many of my callers tell me that I'm a really good listener, and many try to get me to call back. They don't want the relief to end, they want me to be there in the future.

But I am no different to other Samaritan's volunteers, OK well maybe a little. I seem to have a knack of making people feel safe and feel a little better. The woman who was in the process of killing herself had already taken a whole load of pills and had more in front of her. At Samaritan's our aim is to reduce suicide, but we accept the individual's choice, we will not talk someone out of it, but just be there for someone. But being there for someone can make the difference, by the end of the call she was laughing, she had flushed the rest of the pills down the toilet, and decided that it was worth living for one more day. I will literally talk about anything, and one of the things we do is not avoid talking about death and wanting to die. The truth is, like me, most don't want to be dead, they just can't bare the pain anymore. I remember how that feels, it is rare these days I feel it, but I do sometimes. But I also know these days that the feeling will pass, and I know how to care for myself to get myself through those very low moments.

Aime, what the hell has this got to do with the Trade Union I hear you wondering.

Well because I do two things as a Trade Union rep, in my new Trade Union. Yes, I come up with strategies and help with the process and paperwork and my background in HR and employment law is useful, but to be fair could probably be offered by others. But as well, and most of the time more importantly, I stand with people through what is often one of the most painful and emotional experiences they have ever gone through. One filled with taboo. People talk about losing a loved one, they don't talk about getting sacked for gross misconduct. Or being bullied, or being made redundant. I see the gold in their skills and hearts at a time when they feel that no-one can see it. I explain what is going to happen next, and walk with them every step of the way. They can ring me in tears and text me when they are scared or angry, and I can respond to them in an emotionally supportive way. And then I come up with a kick arse legal and strategic plan that gets them the best possible outcome.

I'm not very good at accepting compliments. I was sitting in a bar with a Trade Union member after a difficult meeting. A very senior and amazing woman, she was being treated appallingly by some even more senior men at a leading university. I was helping her navigate through the process, and had met with her before the meeting, and then sat with her during the meeting, taking the lead where necessary, and we were talking afterwards. And then she started turning some of my strategy and compliments back at me and I got very uncomfortable. She laughed, knowing exactly what was going on, and kept bloody talking. She told me how helpful I'd been, how skilled I was, how she was going to tell everyone she knew how good I was.

And I nearly ran.

I squirmed.

I'm much better at taking insults than compliments.

She's kept in touch, and we've become friends, something that sometimes happens with Trade Union clients, it is the intensity of the process.

It's making me uncomfortable just writing this, and I was planning to write about some of our success stories, but now that just feels like boasting, so I'm struggling. But I know that is the good girl stuff creeping in. I'm expected to be excellent at everything I do, but humble and never tell anyone, just let the other people, the men tell everyone about how wonderful they are... even if they aren't.

But I'm fighting it.

OK, compromise, I'll tell you another story first, regain my composure, and come back to the stories of me and the Trade Union but just briefly. I think that is all I can manage for now. I'm sure there will be an opportunity to tell more Trade Union war stories and successes another day. I mean, we are friends now right? I feel like we are, I feel like if you have got this far, we are destined to see more of each other at some point.

I was talking about class, and me being middle class, but my Dad and his family were born very working class (to be fair he's pretty middle class now, but he wasn't born that way).

And class matters, because it sets the context of what you think is possible, and gives you a set of skills. Middle class skills include ordering in posh restaurants and dealing with officials and knowing how to get a good education for your children. But although I see class, I'm not prepared to be bound by it, and I'll happily step around it and enjoy talking to people of all types. One of my current polys is a social work professor and we have long talks about this kind of thing.

My grandfather and grandmother were both strong and active members of the Labour Party (although when Grandma became a business woman she became conservative, and she thought Margaret Thatcher was amazing). My Grandad, George, became one of two full time Trade Union Organisers for the Amalgamated Society of Textile Workers. George's lineage is Irish, and he was always a laid back happy man, who loved to talk. We all get our sociable side from George. He would walk round Leek and collect the subs in cash by hand, and help people out and chat to them, then spend the evening in the working mens club with his mates. He may have been married with four sons, but he pretty much stayed a bachelor in many ways. He was a fabulous Grandad and often babysat after school, happy to watch kids TV with us behind the shop my Grandma ran and owned. Between them my grandparents knew everyone in Leek, and when they both died, the churches were full to bursting for each funeral.

So my family has long been involved in trade unions and been involved with the Labour Party. In fact, George was good friends with Lord Harold Davies, the MP in Leek between 1945 and 1970, so much so that Lord Harold is my Dad's godfather. And well there are many stories there, as Harold became Private Secretary to Harold Wilson and a Privy Councillor, eventually becoming Baron

Davies of Leek, after being sent by Harold Wilson to negotiate between Ho Chi Minh and the Americans in the Vietnam war... and well that is quite a story... but I digress...

I have some interesting stories about being sent to France in my teens to stay with some very unusual people who were unbeknownst to my Mum and Dad, heavily involved with the Communist party... but well that again is another story...

Dad was an active member of the Labour party, and well as kids we just helped out. Dad was the Chair of the Goodmayes and Ilford Labour Party in 1997 and I came back from Uni to help out. It was quite a party that night. Mike Gapes got back in as the Labour Candidate for Ilford South, and of course it was a Labour landslide (it really was quite a party). But one of the most shocking things of the night was watching Linda Perham's face when the results came in. She was the candidate for Ilford North, but with a huge Conservative majority she had not expected to win. She was a full-time librarian, but I watched her face as she realised that she had actually won, and she had to ring her boss to resign. That was a crazy night.

So it isn't all that surprising that when I've not been politically restricted by jobs, I have been an active member of the Labour Party. I have been Treasurer of the local party, and run a prospective MPs social media campaign and even stood as a Labour Councillor (not expecting to win, but I didn't think it was right that people literally couldn't vote Labour).

So, to be fair, the middle class and going to Coopers, and working in HR things is stranger than me setting up a Trade Union to fight for people's rights. But perhaps it does explain my tendency to work in the public sector.

But I have many friends that are Conservatives. And actually I would consider myself a bit of a political mix. My heart is labour, my head is conservative and my soul is green. I actually think if it was even vaguely possible, instead of fighting with each other, if the different parties could work together to help the country to thrive they would be like the most awesome leadership team ever. Just because someone is Labour doesn't mean all their ideas are great, and not all tories are nasty (in fact I think most of them have pretty big hearts they just tend to be workaholics who don't like talking about their feelings and don't always notice their privilege).

And well that leads me nicely back to some of the cases I've had as a Trade Union rep for my HR and Workers Trade Union. HR find me unpredictable but surprisingly helpful. Most of the time they are struggling to deal with a situation, and whichever side I'm on (the employers or the employees) resolving the situation is about finding a way, however messy, to move forward. I've had various Directors of HR refer friends and colleagues to me, after dealing with me supporting a Trade Union Member. I guess I deal with it in some ways as high level diplomacy.

I usually tell people up front what I'm going to attempt to do, and then do it. If the other side comes to the table and is reasonable and fair, then I treat them as such, if they try to just take over and destroy the other side (and many do) then, well I calmly use all that skill and experience, to get the best outcome I can for my member. If the employer gets nasty, then the gloves come off.

ENC said I was scary and supported people too much, well I guess I've just leant into that.

Yes so, I've gone round the houses and distracted you and myself with some stories, but now I need to explain what I've done well, however difficult I find it..

The first Trade Union case I took on, was before I even thought of setting up a Trade Union. I was pregnant with my youngest when my now ex-husband was sacked by his employer after taking six weeks off for depression (this was in the local press at his request so I'm not outing him!). He had only been there a few months, and they tried to pretend they were dismissing him for other reasons. His depression got worse and he didn't have a job. We didn't have enough money to pay for lawyers, so I did the whole case myself, from the paperwork to presenting at the Employment Tribunal (usually done by Barristers). I had my youngest by c-section on 24th December. I spent a week in the Tribunal arguing the case six weeks later, with an almost non-functioning husband who only managed to attend one day at the tribunal, a 6 week old baby and a three year old. Not something I would recommend to anyone.

But we won. I don't tend to go all the way through to Tribunal as part of the Trade Union (there are expert employment Barristers and solicitors who are much better than me), but I learnt a lot, that now helps me when I represent Trade Union members.

I do five things primarily:

1. I listen with kindness and understanding - many Trade Union members I support have never told anyone what is happening, they feel too embarrassed, most don't even tell their partners the full details. My Samaritans training is really useful, I listen without judgement, I am just there for you.
2. I operate then as a soundboard and a strategic partner discussing options, and finding ways forward, using everything that I know about HR, employment law, psychology and poker (employment law is more like poker than you might realise).
3. I go through everything with you. I go to every meeting, I talk to you beforehand, and afterwards. Often in the pub. Nobody should have to go through this alone, and you don't need to. With the HR and Workers Trade Union you are never alone.
4. When people hit the wall and can't do something, I step in and do it for them. The law allows me to act as your representative, and I will never do anything that you don't want me to, but I can talk on your behalf[50]. In one case I am doing right now, it has been so stressful for the Trade Union member (who is heavily pregnant) that all communication now goes through me. I can soften and deal with many of the issues when it is necessary (I don't automatically do this, as it is better to do things with support - but it is useful to know this option is there). I wrote a strong email to her boss about her being a scrooge, it made my member laugh. Laughter eases tension and anxiety. Doing that is a plus.
5. I help you define success. Binary thoughts of winning and losing are often unhelpful. We talk about Bronze, Silver,

Gold and Platinum successes. Platinum is the big win plus the apology and lots of money, but this is rarely achieved. And sometimes a bronze win is simply to know that you can walk away, or that you can speak up, and that feels good, even if no-one listens.

I manage expectations, but to be honest, looking back at my membership successes I have noticed that I have helped more people than I'd thought get Silver, Gold and Platinum wins.

Grievances for racism are really really difficult to get upheld. But I helped one Trade Union member put in a grievance for racism against her boss. After an investigation that crossed continents, the organisation sacked her boss and agreed a compensation package that amounted to around a year's salary (this is a very rare event!).

I undertook a group action against a PLC that was struggling and had stopped paying its staff. It was going bust, but I managed to intervene and get the CEO to undertake and issue redundancy notices to all staff before they liquidated (I wrote the redundancy notices for her - win win). This meant that our members could get government compensation when they went bust and were wound up by the courts.

Sometimes the satisfaction is just in standing up. I helped one person deal with a horrible CEO who had been going round undermining their director's position by telling staff that they thought they weren't great and who agreed. I challenged the CEO's behaviour in the meeting.

The CEO said "I can do what I want".

I responded "Indeed, but that doesn't make it a good idea"

The Director of HR spurted her tea out and couldn't make eye contact, she was desperately trying not to laugh. The CEO just spluttered, they weren't used to anyone standing up to them.

The director who was being bullied had lost their mojo but felt just a little bit better as we talked about what had happened in the pub afterwards. Oh, and I also got them a deal as well, because the CEO just wanted the issue to go away (and she probably wanted me to go away as well...)

You see, I don't want anyone ever to feel scared of me. And I don't try to be scary, honest I don't. But if dodgy bosses don't like the fact that I know my stuff, and I'm not scared of them, then it isn't really my fault if they find me scary now is it?

I've had lots of lovely presents as thank you's from Trade Union clients, from two boxes (98 bars!) of Orange Twirls, to jewellery, meals out (including a trip to Heston Blumenthal's Fat Duck!), flowers and many boxes of Lego, but the nicest thing ever is just the smiles, and the thank yous.

Recently I got the following message from the wife of a member, where I'd helped her husband, her husband's friend and her sister...

"Thanks again for chatting to my little sister... you really helped her and gave her the confidence to face the bastard! X said to Y yesterday he had seen one of the guys from the company and he was saying how formidable you were and that basically everyone at the company is now petrified of you xxx"

As I said, I never set out to scare anyone, honestly... but if that is the way I'm going to be perceived, I guess I might as well lean into it to help my members.

Setting up the Trade Union and supporting people is one of the most satisfying things I have ever done. We are still small, but we are growing, and I'm planning to write some mini courses and guides so that people can get help even if they don't want a representative, or can't afford one, and I'm going to look into creating a war chest where people who have money can fund cases for people who don't have any. And I still take on a few cases personally. I feel like this is part of who I am, it is what I am meant to be doing. And I probably wouldn't have got here if all the shit hadn't gone down at ENC. So, in some ways, maybe I should thank David Oliver. I mean it doesn't excuse his poor behaviour. But his terrible leadership and nasty behaviour was actually what spurred me on to get where I needed to be in the world.

It's a strange old world, isn't it...

Are you ready to empower yourself at work?

To stop being treated like shit and trampled all over?

Are you being unfairly accused of something?

Or do you need help putting in a grievance?

Then get in touch with your new secret weapon.

The HR and Workers Trade Union.

You don't have to do this stuff alone!

Join the HRWTU mailing list by scanning the QR code here ....

Chapter 13
The Kickstart Scheme

The pandemic, lockdown, they seem like forever ago now don't they. Some long lost forgotten dream. It was all so weird that in some ways it is hard to believe it ever actually happened. Did we all have to stay in the house, for what was it in the end months? Did the schools close and parents suddenly had to home school. Did the government really offer to cover the majority of people's salaries while they couldn't get to work? It all seems a bit surreal.

But when the first lockdown was announced in March 2020, I had only been working for myself for less than a year, and suddenly everything was shut. I had started making a name for myself as Ninja HR doing complex investigations, but well, none of that was happening with lock down. Difficult people were just sent home and put on Furlough, problem solved, for the time being at least. So what was I going to do? I needed to earn a living, but I also needed something to do. I volunteered to deliver shopping and prescriptions for people in the village, and that got me out of the house a bit, but it didn't solve the salary problem. But I kept reading about what was going on, and saw it as an opportunity to grow the HR and Workers Trade Union.

Then I came across an announcement for the Kickstart Scheme. Worried that the pandemic was going to plunge a generation of young workers into unemployment the Government wanted to help them. The evidence suggests that young people who are unable to get work for a prolonged period early on in their lives struggle to ever get back on the career paths that others might have had. They miss out on the experiences, but it also knocks their confidence. The government was worried that a whole generation of young people would fall out of employment and into benefits for their whole life, switching from earners to those that needed support, so they created the Kickstart Scheme.

The idea was that the government would pay employers to take on an unemployed young person aged between 16 and 23 for a six month placement. The role needed to be a new role (no filling current vacancies) and needed to be real work. The employers needed to provide training for the young people, not just training to do the job they were doing, but employability support to help them in their career and help them get the next job. In return the employer would get a grant that covered the entire cost of the Kickstarter's salary, and an additional support grant to pay for things like uniform, laptops and the administrative cost of setting up the employability training. It was I believe the most generous salary support grant ever offered by the UK government, and two billion pounds was set aside to fund the scheme (or earmarked, I suspect they probably borrowed the money).

The Department of Work and Pensions (DWP) was given the task of administering the scheme. It was a huge and totally new idea, that needed to go from idea to delivery in a matter of weeks. Usually government grant schemes like this would be years in the creation, with thousands of meetings and hours and documents creating the rules, but there was no time for that. Realising that they were going to struggle to deliver this, the DWP originally announced that the scheme would only be offered to companies that were large enough to take at least 30 Kickstarters, meaning they needed to have at least 300 staff already (as the ratio was determined to be ten current staff to each new Kickstarter). This was set because it was felt that this meant organisations would have the infrastructure, management, and systems to support a whole cohort of trainees. But it was probably also a little bit about finding an easier way to get lots of Kickstarter placements set up easily.

There was a few weeks of large companies announcing they were going to join the scheme then some backtracking as this didn't always play well with the public. The idea of big wealthy companies taking so much government grant funding wasn't popular with the public. And then there was an outcry from smaller businesses. Why could they not got involved? They needed help too.

So, ministers announced that small companies would be able to apply for Kickstart grants to employ just one person, but the DWP wasn't sure they had the resources to deal with all the questions. Larger organisations have HR teams and understand how to run payroll and training programmes and deal with grant requirements, small businesses may not. They created the idea of Kickstart Gateways. Any organisation or group of employers could group together and apply for a Kickstart grant for at least 30 Kickstarters, then the DWP would work with the Gateway directly and the Gateway would then help the smaller employers. The rules for applying for the Gateway were only threefold:

1. The Gateway must already have got employers on board and requests for 30 placements. They needed to do this and organise it themselves.
2. The people running the Gateway must already have experience of running something similar.
3. The employability training programme offered by the Gateway must be approved as being of a sufficient quality.

My company was new, and just me, but I had spent my career running recruitment campaigns, and had been writing, delivering and commissioning training programmes that whole time too. I was also used to dealing with all the bureaucracy and expectations of the public sector, or as my friend called me I was the "public sector whisperer" so I could do this couldn't I?

In fact, I was far more confident of my ability to set this up and deliver it than I was of being able to find customers who would trust me to be their Gateway. Overnight websites appeared and HR companies and recruitment agencies and even some local authorities started looking to find companies to support so they could get approved as a Gateway. I saw all the glossy websites and felt defeated. I know I could do this, but I couldn't compete with all their infrastructures, and I didn't know how to sell and I didn't know how to attract customers. I felt defeated, and I hadn't even begun. I felt like I was a fraud and shouldn't have even thought about doing this. I gave up before I had even tried.

But then my sister called me. My brother in law and her had set up a company SYF Massage, and they wanted to get a Kickstarter, but they realised they needed a Gateway. My sister said something like

"Surely you could help us do this Aime, sounds like your kind of thing, and might be fun".

Oh bollocks, now my little sister, who I adore and would go through fire and hell for, had asked me to help, I was going to have to do this. Time to put on those big girl pants again.

But a lifetime of delivering impossible projects in impossible situations in the public sector, and a deep well of resilience (or is it bloody minded stubbornness? I'm not sure I can tell the difference anymore), and well I didn't have anything better to do. So I used an old coaching tip and flipped the question.

Knowing what I know and with the resources I had, how could I do this?

It is a great question, it flips the mind from what is a problem, to looking for a solution.

Social media, that was the solution. I might not have any customers yet, or a website, but I had social media accounts, and I knew they could be used to get customers. I mean essentially social media is a window into everyone's phone right?

OK, but I didn't know anything about social media. I'd pretty much avoided it, for the same reason I gave up going to staff Christmas parties (plenty of stories there... including one about an HR Director and some photos...). I can't unsee things and as an HR professional if I see a friend or colleague doing something completely inappropriate on social media I'll have to investigate it and I don't want to do that. Plus, you know, middle class professionals don't share what they are eating for dinner to the world, that is all very crass and you know cheap (I know no one ever says that out loud).

But well I didn't think like that, I think everyone is awesome, and I'm not judgemental, and I love some of the content I was seeing on social media. And suddenly some massive disadvantages in my career switched to being advantages.

a) I love rolling my sleeves up and learning practically - it is essentially just me playing (and did you know you learn much more quickly and much more effectively if you are playing - it's why everyone wants to gamify everything right now).

b) I've always been that overly chatty person who asks a dozen questions at every training session, talks to everyone, is generally very informal and puts emojis in her professional emails.

c) I'm a pretty open person. Whilst very few people get REALLY close, I'll tell people on the bus most of my life story.

I've had numerous people tell me off over the years, from professors to bosses that my style of communication is "too friendly, not austere enough Aime, too chatty," "you really really shouldn't put emojis in work emails Aime" - that kind of thing.

But hold on a second, social media is all about posting and seeing what works, and chatting with everyone, commenting all over the place and being open about your life.

So I took a big deep breath, and put out on social media that I was going to be a Gateway. And then I ran away and nearly threw up and buried myself in repeat episodes of Star Trek and anything bingeable (my go to retreat mechanism when I feel vulnerable and overexposed).

And then I emerged a week later and got on with the work at hand. I started working out how this scheme could work in practice, and started talking about it on social media.

I arranged discovery calls, and within a few weeks I had persuaded enough companies to go with me as their Kickstart Gateway to be able to submit an application to the DWP for a request for 30 Kickstart Placement Grants.

Turns out as long as I really believe in something, I'm pretty good at sales.

I just can't sell things I don't believe in!

It was really hard, and totally overwhelming, but I just kept at it anyway. I knew I could do this; I knew I could do it well, I just had to get through the sales bit, and keep going. A bit like the HR and Workers Trade Union, this was only going to work if I believed it would work and tried to make it work.

I found out on 2nd December 2020 that we had been accepted, the one-year anniversary of me setting up the HR and Workers Trade Union - it was a special day!

Eighty percent of Gateway applicants were turned down. There was a lot of anger, and questions in the media and online. But my solid public sector background had won out. I knew what they wanted from me, and I knew how to create a process and training programme that they would sign off. So, Ninja HR became a Kickstart Gateway!

And once I had been accepted there really wasn't much explanation about what would happen next. Throughout my application process I had been in contact with the fabulous DWP local rep. To be honest we both learnt how it worked as we went along. We didn't talk often, but I enjoyed our conversations. We tried to support each other, we were in this together.

Well, I was used to a blank sheet of paper. So, I just made it work, I created processes and built a team. When no one knew what was happening, or how, I just worked something out and talked with people and made it work. Most Kickstart Gateways failed in the first few weeks and months, but we were on a roll. We scaled up from just me to a team of 10 in a few months. I was initially offered a grant of just over £1 million to work with the initial fifteen employers. As cohort one went so successfully, we gained a further 75 employers and our grant rose to over £3million. In total we helped to create 237 new jobs for young people, supporting all of those employers and delivering employability training. In our busiest month, the gross income to my company was over £40,000.

It was always a pandemic and temporary project, so having scaled up and delivered so much, it was soon time to scale back down again. I hated having to tell the team when the government finally announced they were closing the doors to new applications. They all rang me afterwards to check I was OK and to reassure me that they knew this was going to happen. I am still very very close friends with all of them. It was quite a ride. But an extra special thank you has to go to Milly Harding. She stepped in and ran the team and became my Chief Operating Officer. Without her, and the rest of the team (including the amazing Kelly Allen who is now one of my business partners - who did all the Kickstart admin!).

And of course, we had our own Kickstart success story. The fabulous Juliette Rees joined us as a Kickstarter herself, helping us to recruit others and support them. When she left, she became an international recruitment consultant, and she is now a Senior Recruitment Consultant based in France (she speaks fluent French amongst other talents). To anyone that assumes that all unemployed people must be lazy and stupid, Juliette is the proof that this is not the case. She has a degree in International Politics and did her year out working at the UN. She was amazing at what she did, she'd just graduated at a very tough time. She came with us the night we won the Niche Award because I wanted the whole team to celebrate our hard work and when she left, she wrote me a lovely email:

November 9 2021

Subject: To the best boss ever!

Hi Aime,

I hope you're well!!!

I know Tom has mentioned that I'm leaving, but I just wanted to drop you a quick line to say thank you for everything! My time at Ninja HR has honestly been so amazing, everyone has been an absolute to delight to work with (and party with).

I also just wanted to thank you for letting me be part of your fantastic team, from networking lunches to awards evening - all I can say is I'm proud to have been part of it. I've loved every minute and have learnt a heck of a lot and I really hope our paths cross again in the future! If you're ever in London and are in need of a pint/G&T you have my number!

Sending you lots of love and wishing you all the best and success going forward!!!!

Will miss you all terribly xxx

Kind regards

Juliette

I'm not sure she'll ever know how much that email meant to me. She didn't know how hard it was to pick myself up off the floor and build something from nothing after being treated so badly at ENC.

I got dozens of thank you letters and gifts and messages from clients and Kickstarters. And the DWP was very pleased too. We ended up being one of the most successful small Gateway's in the UK and were more successful at getting new clients and placing young people successfully than most of the larger Gateway's (many were booted out of the scheme early).

But just as I was wrapping up the scheme, and it was back down to just me, one client got nasty.

Most of the companies I had screened personally (there were some pretty tough checks to get through via the DWP, and I didn't want to be responsible for delivering in organisations that didn't have the right values). I had been given a lot of delegated responsibility by the DWP and I took that seriously.

Like many pandemic schemes it was more about getting the money out first and then checking the paperwork afterwards. As the scheme drew to a close, I started working with our clients to make sure that they had done the right things, evidenced their grant expenditure etc. I wrote to one client, lets call them BB Ltd on 1st July 2021 asking them to get in touch and send me some details about what they had been up to and evidence of payments to staff, training undertaken etc.

I held off the last payments until I received the confirmations from clients. The way the money was structured I was the grant recipient which meant I had to make sure the money was spent properly, otherwise it could be reclaimed by the DWP from me. I didn't want a situation where I had given it out, only for the DWP to claim it back from me. That was a massive financially liability.

All the other companies had no problem getting in touch, but I hadn't spoken to the Director of BB Ltd, they had come to me via an HR colleague, who had asked for some help when her company and BB Ltd had failed in their joint bid to become a Gateway. Not wanting them to miss out I supported them by putting in the grants claims via our Gateway, only holding back £300 in administrative costs per placement (not the full £1,800 which paid for the training and all the HR as well). The deal was that they should be able to do things themselves, and just need a little oversight from me. I had already sent them more than £30,000 in grant funding but held back the last £9,000.

They didn't respond for four months, then I got a threatening call from the Director, who I had never spoken to before that day telling me I'd better pay up now, or else.

Delightful.

He didn't seem to have got the email of 1st July, so I forwarded it to him, and asked him not to speak to me like that again.

He didn't fancy doing any of the things I'd asked and said my email was not very nice. Here is my email... I'll let you decide whether it is nice or not.

Hi D!

I hope that you are well and business is good.

I'm sending this email to you as you have been supporting BB Ltd and their clients...

It has been my pleasure to be able to be able to support small companies such as yourself to get access to Kickstart grant funding after the shock to us all that was the pandemic.

This scheme was set up quickly and has evolved as it has gone along. Most of the time you have not seen any of this as we have acted as the go-between between yourselves and the DWP. As we near the end of the scheme, the DWP appears to be attempting to claw back as much money as it can. They appear to be looking through the details of payments to see whether any errors have been made. They have already sent invoices to reclaim some funds. I'd hoped they would be a bit more generous but c'est la vie.

In a bid to ensure that all our customers can retain as much of the grant funding as possible, I want to try and get ahead of the possible requirements/objections of the DWP. I am also realistic that it is easier to not receive money than it is to pay it back, so as the final few payments are coming through we are double checking things carefully. I've also asked the DWP for extended repayment terms so that if you do have to pay anything back it can be done so in a gradual fashion as I appreciate that any money received by you, you will most likely have presumed you could keep.

So, to assist me to assist you in the smooth receipt of final payments, and retention of payments you have already received please can you send through the documents I've requested below.

We have more than 90 companies we have facilitated receipt of the Kickstart funding, and it will take time to review and process the paperwork, so please bear with us. We will release final funding as soon as all of the checks have been made and cleared, and will operate a first come first served approach, so the quicker you get all your paperwork back the quicker you'll get your final payments! I'll try to be as pragmatic as I can with what evidence you send, but ultimately the DWP will be checking this, so I'll need to have in mind that they will be the ultimate arbitrators not me, so please have this in mind when you consider what you send through. I don't have a list or rules about what is acceptable, but more than 20 years working in the public sector has given me a pretty good idea of what they want.

Unfortunately, I have had the odd company during our time as a Gateway who has been quite rude, threatening and demanding in their interactions with me and my team. The majority however have been an absolute delight though, so thank you. So fair warning: rude, threatening, demanding, aggressive and inappropriate behaviour towards me or any of my team (in email, letters or over the phone) will not result in a quicker/better response but result in your paperwork being put at the bottom of the pile to be dealt with when everyone else's has been resolved.

I can foresee that I may get 100s of very specific questions about formats and what exactly do I want and what is acceptable. I'm not going to try to quantify this as the DWP will create it's own rules (even if they don't share them). If in doubt simply send me your best shot, and if I need more I'll ask for it. So just to reiterate, if you ask questions about what is OK, I'm not going to answer, just send through what you've got, preferably in one batch via email or one of the sharing platforms. The easier you make it for me to review, the quicker it will get done.

Also, again as no doubt I'll get asked, this does not mean I'm stopping all payments, but consider that your last payment (or possibly two if I think there may be bigger issues) for each Kickstarter will be slightly delayed pending receipt of your paperwork. I know this is inconvenient, but as I've said, I hoped the DWP would have been a little more generous, but as this doesn't seem to be their approach, I am simply going to have to go with it, and so are you I'm afraid.

OK so what am I looking for. Well for every Kickstart employee you have received any funding for (even if it was just the support grant) you will need to provide the following:

1. A copy of all their payslips.

2. Evidence of what training and development you have done to support them as per the terms of the grant (this may simply be listing the courses they have attended that we have delivered, but can also include other training, and their use of the PDB, if you have undertaken the development yourself I will need some evidence of what

was done, when, by who and what the outcome was). I don't need huge amounts of detail, if you're not sure, submit what you've got and I'll have a look and then get back to you if I need more. Again, don't worry if not every t was crossed and i dotted, I'm not looking for perfection, I'm looking for each Kickstarter receiving some support.

3. Receipts for what you have spent the support grant on (the grant rules require it to have been spent on the individual) – there is more detail in the Facebook group, and you can include management time you have spent supporting them, or things like asking your accountant to do work. I'm not looking for perfection here, just a logical qualification of how you have spent the money.

4. The personal mobile phone number of each Kickstarter (obviously re: GDPR you should let them know you are doing this and that I may call). I will call a percentage of Kickstarters to verify the above information. I know that not all placements have gone well. I've been round the block or two, I'm not looking for a glowing report (although that would be nice) and if I get any negative feedback I will come back to you first (I am well aware there are always two sides to every story). Simply getting a negative response from a Kickstarter will not necessarily be a problem (although again I hope that this will be very rare). I will be more concerned if I simply get no response at all…

That's it for now. I wish I could absolutely guarantee that I will not have to ask for any more, but that simply isn't how this scheme has evolved. Those of you in cohort 1 will know that I asked for person specifications, only for the DWP to create their own and give it to us to fill out at the last minute…

Kind regards

Aime

He refused to send me any information, instead deciding to go on social media and put on various posts that I was a fraud, and sending me messages saying and I quote

"Hey Aime, your fraud isn't going away, how do you want to resolve?".

I blocked him and deleted the messages from my socials. I told him I would deal with him via email only, and I would process his final payments, but only when he had done what I had asked him to (all things that were set out in the agreement).

A few months later I got a strong letter from a debt collection agency telling me I had to pay BB Ltd £15,000. I politely emailed them to explain that it wasn't a debt, but a grant, and that BB Ltd hadn't complied with the agreement they had signed, which clearly stated that I could withhold and even require repayment of grant money. I suggested that maybe they talk to BB Ltd and that their best bet was to simply send what I had asked. I had put aside the money and would hold it as such till this was resolved.

It went quiet again. Then a few months later I got a strong letter from a big London Solicitor's firm telling me that I must now pay £22,000 within seven days, and if I didn't they would petition the court to wind up my company for failing to pay a debt.

Again, I politely said no.

I don't like being bullied.

Even if the bullies come with legal degrees and from large firms with thousands of lawyers, seventeen offices and an annual turnover of more than £200 million.

They started legal processes to wind up my company, and I was served notice. This works pretty much like on TV. An officer of the court is sent out with documents, and they have to be legally served to the person.

It is meant to be intimidating.

It is.

Notice was published, and a fabulous Nigel from www.fastspeedslegals.co.uk called me up to offer to help. For a one off fee he offered to support me via his firm through this process. He suggested that I should offer to pay a proportion of the amount. I explained the situation, and said that I wasn't going to pay them on principle. He said that almost no one ever challenged a petition to wind up a company, that it was notoriously difficult to win, and that it would probably cost me at least £10,000 to put in all the paperwork. He offered to support me through the initial hearing, where he said I would be put on a list of dozens of companies, and they might just ignore me and wind up the company or hear my case on the spot or delay.

So, I did all the paperwork myself (much cheaper) and I went up to Leeds. The Judge postponed the case and listed it for a half day hearing a few months later.

Then something rather bizarre happened.

I was at a party, and I was introduced to a Partner in the legal firm that was helping BB Ltd to sue me. I looked him up afterwards and he was actually a partner in their Insolvency team. So, it was actually his team that were suing me. He hadn't worked out who I was I don't think (totally out of context to be fair). I contacted the lawyer at the big firm and explained what had happened.

The lawyer rang me up directly a few days later. In itself odd as I now had a lawyer representing me (albeit I was doing the paperwork myself). That conversation was horrible. Basically he tried to tell me I didn't understand the Kickstart scheme, and was just being silly, that I should stop messing about and just pay up. If I didn't they would force my company to be closed and tell the insolvency practitioner to investigate me for fraud. It was a very clear threat. Pay up or they would throw the full force of their law firm at me and force my company to fold, then suggest that I should be struck off as a Director. He also suggested that it was the DWP in charge not me, he inferred that I was basically just a glorified administrator, and I should just do as I was told.

I kept my calm on the phone, but said no. That perhaps he had misunderstood the Kickstart scheme, and that this wasn't a debt and that I didn't like bullies.

Then I put down the phone and burst into tears.

Seriously, again?

Is it really my fault?

But sod it, again it wasn't about me. This is fairly standard practice to threaten smaller companies with a winding up petition. Most, scared out of their wits, pay up, and not just whatever the original request was, but all the legal costs too.

Then it got really bizarre. You know that partner that I met at a party, who I'd told his firm about the potential conflict.

In the middle of the night a few weeks later he sent me some provocative personal messages.

OK now this was just getting weird. I contacted my legal team. They said that the lawyer shouldn't have contacted me directly, and that the partner should definitely not have messaged me once I'd explained to his team that there was a conflict (the messages were after the email to the firm). They said that this was one of the reasons solicitors get a bad name and suggested that I make a complaint to the Solicitors Regulation Authority.

So, I did just that.

And prepared for my day in court.

I was scared shitless. And pissed off (I had to miss a Coopers event I had helped to organise where we had commissioned our very own beer because I had to be in Leeds in court arguing to protect my company from being wound up).

I mean I know a fair bit about employment law, but this was insolvency law, a very specialist area. I had read up, but it was still going to be difficult. Even most solicitors don't present cases in court, this is left to Barristers, a tough career choice that requires lots of study and practice. I mean I know I had a law degree, and had almost become a Barrister, but that isn't quite the same as going into court and doing what a Barrister does, in front of a Judge, up against a real Barrister, and trying to fight for everything you have spent several years building. I knew that my chances of winning were miniscule, but well, I just had to do this didn't I?

The big legal firm put in a last-minute request for even more costs, and also a statement saying that they hadn't done anything wrong. It turned out that the first lawyer hadn't actually raised the issue of me meeting the partner, because basically he thought I was making it up. He thought it wasn't really possible that I had met him, and therefore didn't tell anyone, including the partner.

Ah, well that explains the message. Not some sort of weird bullying, just common to garden flirting, or maybe even a mistake. I mean it's quite hard to send a message accidentally on LinkedIn messages as you have to select the photo of the person you are sending it to first, but it was two in the morning so I guess it could have been a mistake rather than harassment. I kind of felt sorry for him, he was probably wondering what the hell was going on, and the SRA investigation could be shock if this junior lawyer had literally told him nothing...

So, I was in court in Leeds, wearing my best black shirt dress and my patent leather DMs (but with black tights, not rainbow coloured ones, this is court after all). I got a compliment from the court Usher about my shoes, and got chatted up by a lovely male Barrister as I was waiting, which did some to elevate the stress. Seriously I was just sitting there!

It was one of the hardest things I have ever done. The big legal firm had sent a Barrister, it was just me and them and the Judge.

I did my best.

It stretched my brain and emotional resilience beyond breaking point. I was so far from my comfort zone I was on another planet, but I just kept going.

The Judge summed up all the legal decisions and complimented both of us for our commendably professional approach to the situation. It seemed to be going well, but she was going through all the legal precedents and her reasons and hadn't given her outcome. It seemed to take forever.

Then she finally gave her judgement.

She threw out the petition to close my company.

I was still in business.

And she threw out the request for legal fees.

I had won.

Against all the odds, against the threats from BB Ltd and the massive legal firm, their team of solicitors and barristers.

Little old me had won.

I wanted to burst into tears right there with relief.

I managed to make it outside first.

The relief was palpable.

I cried for about half an hour, not able to move, in total shock.

My client, and a massive legal company had thrown all their weight and legal knowledge at me, and I had defended myself, and won.

That does not happen very often.

I bought myself a doughnut to celebrate and went home.

I slept well that night.

I think that might have been the hardest thing I have ever done (and I had two difficult births!).

The Solicitor's Regulation Authority say that they will respond to complaints within a month. After three months, I had heard nothing so I chased them.

When I got the response back I was livid. They had interviewed both of the lawyers, but not me, and the response was incredibly patronising. Apparently, the partner had inferred that I had somehow made up the screenshots. WTF. It is one thing to say that it was a mistake, but to suggest that he didn't send the messages...

The exact words of the SRA were *"X has had sight of the screenshot you have provided and can only state that if this message was indeed sent by him, then it must have been a mistake (and perhaps a message intended for a different recipient). As X has no record or recollection of this message, he cannot comment any further..."*

Hmm, what do you think of that...?

And with regard to the other lawyer, it was accepted that he called me. The SRA's response to this was and I quote:

"Whilst I'm appreciate the nature of the phone call may have caused you and your team member hurt [what team member?] we do not consider that our threshold test for what we would ordinarily constitute as intimidating or threatening correspondence has been met".

They didn't say what that threshold was or ask me what had happened in the phone call, they just asked the lawyer.

They assumed I was a litigant in person (which I hadn't been at the time of the phone call) and they didn't even bother to speak to me or hear my side of the story.

They just basically believed the lawyers, and their argument seems to be that they were allowed to cause hurt and that was OK. I think the presumption is simply that this is the way things are done.

Well maybe it is the way things have been done.

But it needs to stop.

I respect that people should have the opportunity to raise matters in court. But threatening behaviour and legal intimidation shouldn't be OK.

I had stood up for myself and won.

But some small business owners might have paid their demand for £25,000 simply because they were scared. And sending nasty messages and making unpleasant phone calls and sending harassing messages. Why does the Solicitor's Regulatory Authority think that this is OK?

Now lots of lawyers are kind, and fair and would never dream of behaving in such a way. But unfortunately, it appears that the SRA doesn't set particularly high standards of behaviour. I wasn't expecting them to be sacked or barred.

I was expecting to be heard fairly, within the timescales they had set, and to receive an apology.

But it is all done now.

And well, I guess they might have been a little bit annoyed that they had spent so much time and legal fees (including the £2,700 court fees) and then lost against little old me...

But I shall not dwell on one bad customer. Being a Kickstart Gateway was an amazing experience. It was amazing to help so many young people, to give them an opportunity to get a job when they were struggling. It felt good to be able to enable small businesses and charities to get government funding during a pandemic. And I enjoyed creating a great team.

It turns out, that without limitations, and bullying bosses who want to keep me small, I'm actually able to achieve quite a lot!

So that is two wins to me. A brand-new Trade Union, and a success as a Kickstart Gateway, scaling to a turnover of more than £2 million in my second year of business (very few businesses ever achieve this, and an even smaller number of female led businesses).

But you know me, that wasn't all I've been up to over the last few years...

Chapter 14
Beyond HR

I think we are friends now. Or at the very least if you've read this far you are curious. And you've seen under the bonnet as such. I've let you into both my world and my brain.

But I'm still a bit cautious about telling you a bit more. You see I've learnt that being fairly open with people can be quite a positive thing. But if I tell people too much, they reject me. They reject me because I'm too different. This lovely connection that we've built is broken because I suddenly feel too far from them, I'm too different, too strange, and I guess sometimes people either feel like I'm lying, or boasting, or if they believe me there is that look in their eyes. That moment when they realise that maybe I'm not lying I just understand the world a little differently and that has advantages. But then for most there is that moment where when they find me intimidating and they are gone, and I'm on my own again.

I've had a couple of weeks off writing, partly because I've been doing other things, but if I'm honest, mainly because I've been trying to work out how honest to be. I've been thinking and reading and sleeping. A lot. My dreams have been incredibly vivid.

But I've made a decision.

I'm just going to be me.

I don't want to be this lonely anymore.

I have spent every moment of my life feeling completely isolated.

Sure, those who know me know I'm a very sociable person, with lots of friends, and a large loving family.

But let me ask you. What does a capable woman do when she feels completely isolated?

She tries to find connections. She learns how to get closer to people.

I don't want to feel isolated. I want to feel that at least one person in the world understands me or sees me.

But I've never really had that. I mean I've got close but, well I have been hiding too much to ever truly be seen.

And I'm also very scared of being rejected. Because if I truly open up and get rejected by everyone then it is game over.

It occurs to me that I might live out my entire life and never truly feel connected to anyone.

And I don't want any of those that are close to me to believe that I don't love those connections or feel close to you. I do, you are.

This is all about me being scared to drop that final curtain.

To be fair, the odd person more recently has tried to get me to trust them, and well it has been a difficult process.

They say that extreme independence is a trust issue.

But I'm also an optimist at heart, so I want to believe it is possible for me to be less scared and less alone.

So, I am trying, and I am making some progress.

So, what the hell does this have to do with HR Aime, you might be wondering?

Well, a lot.

Strolling through Barcelona with my sister a few years ago, the sunshine warming our backs as we wandered back into the city from the Gaudi museum, we were talking about many things. We were meandering and perhaps it was the unusual architecture of Gaudi that spurred the conversation, or the cocktails, but we were talking about the nature of work and reality.

When I am at work, and I am given a problem, I want to fix it. So does she. But we were talking about the fact that actually most people don't want to fix the problem.

It seems obvious doesn't it. If you work in the public sector, and you get given a piece of work, no matter how hard, then you just keep going till you fix it don't you? No matter how wrong it goes, how difficult it is, how exhausted you are, you just keep going. And you don't kid yourself, you test the solution to see if it actually works, before you declare a success.

This is how we were brought up. Dad was a Science teacher before he became an Educational Psychologist, and came from a very practical family. One of his brother's is an engineer and runs the last plumbing manufacturing factory in the UK, there are so few people that can do what he does now that the Italian machine manufacturers who manufacture the plant in the factory send engineers to him for training, the other brother is a master potter (he designs the challenges on the Great Pottery Throw down amongst other things). As kids Dad would always teach us the science behind how things worked, and even to this day we often talk about science round the dining room table (although we might also talk about farting or giggle about the silliest thing, I tend to laugh so much I cry and almost throw up when I'm with them all for an extended time, which is a few times a year - we are all going on holiday for a week, six weeks on Wednesday and I am SO excited).

So my sis and I were talking about how we'd realised that not everyone went at a problem with the determination to fix it, and well that was weird and we didn't understand why.

I've thought about that conversation a lot, and I think I've found the why.

So Freud, amongst lots of rubbish that he spouted, did come up with some good ideas that seem to have stuck both in academia and the minds of the general population. The subconscious being one of them (and psychoanalysis). And you have probably heard of the ego, which he talked a lot about. The ego is our sense of self, and it likes to believe that it is awesome. We will do a lot to make ourselves feel good enough (including trying to be good girls). His amazing daughter, Anna Freud is less well known, she was a school teacher and then a psychoanalyst who specialised in supporting and understanding children. But you have probably heard of her most famous contribution to psychology; defence mechanisms. She suggested that the ego couldn't cope with all of the attacks on it, so to protect ourselves we defend. We might deny something is happening, or blame someone else, or bury ourselves in a project so we don't have to think about the unpleasant thing. She suggested that all of us use these defence mechanisms about ten times a day. They are good short term survival strategies, but they don't allow personal growth or a focus on actually fixing the problem in the longer term.

I believe, defence mechanisms are the reason there are so many plans and meetings and strategy sessions.

If a senior manager is faced with a really difficult intractable problem, if they organise a meeting and create a plan it feels like they have made excellent progress, so their ego is satisfied.

But of course that is just the beginning of the process of change. A meeting and a plan are not change themselves.

But managers console themselves feeling that talking about the problem and making a plan is almost as good as fixing the problem.

It may feel good.

But the problem isn't fixed.

Then it is easier to either pretend the problem has gone away, or blame someone else.

Instead of taking responsibility for getting the real work done.

To really put yourself out there and try to do things is painful and often doesn't work, no matter how hard you try. Theodore Roosevelt is famous for the following quote, often called the man in the arena

"It is not the critic who counts, not the man who points out how the strong man stumbles, or where the doer of deeds could have done them better. The credit belongs to the man who is actually in the arena, whose face is marred by dust and sweat and blood; who strives valiantly; who errs, who comes short again, and again, because there is no effort without error and shortcoming; who does actually strive to do the deeds; who knows great enthusiasms, the great devotions; who spends himself in a worthy cause; who at the best knows in the end the triumph of high achievement, and who at the worst, if he fails, at least fails while daring greatly, so that his place shall never be with those cold and timid souls who neither know victory nor defeat."

You see it is easy to talk about stuff, and make plans, and have meetings. Actually getting things done, is harder, and messier, and doesn't always work. Which is why Roosevelt was so kind to the man in the arena.

Stirring stuff, but also very scary.

I tell people that I'm not competitive, that is a little disingenuous, what I really mean is that I'm only competitive when things matter to me. So I don't mind losing at sport and I'm not invested in one team or the other winning, I hate conflict and just want everyone to be happy. But this is purely for selfish reasons, I'm an empath, and by that I just mean that I'm reasonably good at reading other people's emotions and imagining what it might be to walk in their shoes, the more I learn about people and the world, the more I understand, the better I read people and the more I therefore empathise with.

It is incredibly painful being an empath. Because on some level I feel pain when other people feel pain. It is much less obviously, but it is triggered by lots of people, and my brain gets flooded with pain because of mirror neurons (but also joy and laughter from time to time). I want to make other people around me happy OK, because it stops it being painful for me. Learning to sit in someone else's pain and not try to fix the situation has been the most difficult thing I have ever done. I just want to fix it and stop the pain.

So what the hell Aime does this have to do with HR you are probably thinking at this point.

Well, so, most people's egos mean that they avoid solving situations. My ego forces me to keep trying, because it is who I am, learnt long ago, probably when I was a baby, because to really fix things is the ultimate buzz, and I also want to stop other people hurting and make them happy, because that means the pain stops, temporarily at least. Which is why I'm not competitive, because if I win and you lose that hurts. I'll do almost anything to try and find a way we can both win, I might even lose on purpose so you can win, because that is easier for me to bear.

So basically I am incredibly motivated to actually fix things, rather than pretend to fix things (although I wish I could con my own brain sometimes to believe something is good enough the way so many people seem to do).

So what the flying fuck has this got to do with HR?

Well HR mainly doesn't work.

It is a process to make the people in charge (managers) feel OK about what they want to do anyway.

And the policies and procedures mainly just allow the people in charge to feel that they did the right thing in the right way even if it didn't work very well and they did it for all the wrong reasons. They are more about justification, than about managing people well. By the time someone has put in a grievance the relationship has probably already been destroyed beyond repair.

I remember 20 years ago when I was working in the private sector, a manager asked me to dismiss a black guy. I asked why? And he said, just find a way, find some reason to get rid of him. Basically, they wanted to sack him because he was black, but wanted me to find a way to sack him that looked like he was being sacked for an entirely different reason.

"You can do that can't you Aime, find a way to dismiss him that will look OK and won't get us into trouble".

I sat at my desk for hours after that conversation. Of course I could. I know exactly how to dismiss anyone. You just find their greatest weakness and then use it against them in a systematic way using the policies procedures and employment law (you can see why some people think I'm scary). Everyone is flawed, it sometimes takes time, but it isn't that hard. In my whole career I've only had one decision I've ever handled where there was even an appeal, not a single one has ever even had a tribunal lodged, let alone gone to tribunal, or lost. Degrees in law, psychology and a masters in HR plus well, I'm just good at this stuff – that's why I'm

The Employment Genie.

I guess it was the first moment I realised I had professional power. I could use my knowledge and experience, but I was also being put into a position where my employer, someone who had huge power over me, was putting me under pressure to do something I knew was wrong. I was 25, I had a fiancée and a mortgage.

What the fuck was I supposed to do.

I said no, handed my notice in and walked out.

I then sat on a bench outside Liverpool Street station and cried for two hours before I went home. How the fuck was I going to pay the bills? How much would my bloody-mindedness cost me? Should I have just done what they told me? What would you have done?

I don't blame the person who might have just sacked the person and done as they are told. We are not to blame for the system that is around us. If you do something like that to save yourself, I understand, and I don't think less of you. If I'm honest I kind of wished I had just sacked him. But actually it turned out alright... I temped for a bit, and then got a maternity cover for an HR officer at Thurrock Council, down the road from where we lived, and met the best manager I've ever had, and learnt about the public sector and social services and felt useful and appreciated. But I didn't know that the day I sat on that bench crying.

And the courts and employment tribunals. I don't think they work very well either. They are not terrible, they do create some justice, and there are some amazing people that do amazing jobs. Lord Denning and Baroness Hale being particularly amazing at actually changing the law and interpreting it in such a way as to make it really do what it says on the box. But most of the time the legal system is just a way to make the white men in power feel good that they are nice people and they have a fair system, and that well if it doesn't work out then that must be because someone didn't deserve to win, or was guilty. That is the problem, whole systems can get defensive and protect themselves by suggesting that they are pure as the driven snow, and that everything works. But to be fair the good people within the system understand that it is a lot greyer and messier than that. And yes I'm using white and black references, because the system is sexist and racist.

Once upon a time I was going to be a Barrister. I did several mini pupillages[52] in one I was with a fabulous black Barrister. I'd already done another mini pupillage in a criminal and civil rights chambers, but I just couldn't stomach that line of work. I'd been involved in three cases. The first was a case where two youngsters had slashed the faces of strangers in a public place. They were only fifteen, but as we talked to them, I saw how their lawyers were essentially coaching them to blame the one eighteen year old who was with them who wasn't their client. He was an adult, but it was clear these young lads knew exactly what they were doing, and to be honest I think it was the only time I've ever been in the physical room with sociopaths (well that I know of anyway). I didn't want to use any skills and knowledge I had to do this kind of thing. Next case, was a rape defence. They put me in a room with all the background paperwork and told me to find things about the victim that they could use in court to undermine her testimony. Oh fuck, I didn't want to do that. I read through the story of her life, and I could only feel for her. I just couldn't do it. At that point I had pretty much decided that I couldn't be a criminal Barrister, although I did vaguely consider going into prosecution. I realised I probably couldn't live with myself if I couldn't manage to get a defendant I believed was guilty convicted. As I stood in the beautiful surroundings in the Inns of court saying my goodbyes a Barrister walked through the corridor in tears. Shocked I asked what had happened. He was someone who specialised in human rights law and he had missed his plane. Hearing about his delay, the country involved had executed his client in a rush before he got there, and he blamed himself for their death.

Fuck, I did not have the stomach for this.

So my next pupillage was in a chambers that specialised in civil cases. I had spent the day in court where the Barrister who was looking after me was arguing about what documents should be in the core bundle (basically the papers) for a long upcoming case about whether or not a golf course had been built properly or not.

I was sitting at the back of the court.

It was boring.

I fell asleep.

I awoke sometime later to find the Judge smiling at me with sympathy.

Sometimes law is just boring. I think he was as bored as I was.

As we walked back through the narrow streets, a phone call came through, the barrister had won a big case. He was as pleased as punch and started talking about what he was going to do with the bonus he had just earned. It was more money than I could imagine, so I was somewhat surprised when we walked past his car on the way to the station. It was an old battered car probably only worth a £1,000. Being probably more blunt than was socially acceptable, I asked him why he didn't have a posher car.

With a sigh, the excitement of winning the case seeming to suddenly disappear as if I had deflated the balloon of his joy, his demeanour and face changed and his body slumped.

He told me that he had had a top of the range black BMW, but he kept getting stopped on his way to court. The police kept thinking he must be a drug dealer, because well he was black and in a posh car, or that he had stolen the car. He had several people tell him he was lying when he said he was a barrister and that he would be late for court. They laughed at him, and when he showed them his wig, they just suggested he stole that as well as the car.

After being stopped numerous times, and even being late for court because of it once, he sold his car and just bought a cheap one. No one had stopped him since.

If at this point you are feeling a little deflated, please don't. You see there is always hope. HR and the law might be a bit of a mess, but there are some amazing people working in these fields who make it work anyway.

And that is why I call it Beyond HR. I do what the best HR practitioners do. I take all the laws, the rules, the expectations, the policies and I find a way to make it work anyway. I add to the things I learnt in my HR MA, including understanding people and what they need, marketing, process redesign. I work out what the client wants, but then deliver it in a way that is OK for everyone, assuming that the ask isn't completely unethical in the first place. And I call this Beyond HR.

To clients it looks like magic, to staff it makes me look like a saviour. But I'm neither a magician or anyone's saviour. I just want things to work, so I find ways to take impossible situations and find ways through. We respect the individual, their needs, their feelings, but also recognise that the employer needs something too,

I'm helping a friend with a staffing matter this week, it's been a tough situation, but I've helped her through it. She has a background in marketing, like high level amazing stuff with mega brands. She was saying that I should market what I do, because it is so different and so great. You see I walk with people and help them. I don't give them a thousand policies or documents, we discuss options, and I give advice and then I write the letter and go to the meeting with them. And every time something happens, we talk and plan what to do next. I do make suggestions, but I never tell people what to do, because it isn't up to me. Every person has their own personal thoughts about risk and what they want to do, whether they would rather spend time or money, take a risk now, or a risk later. I just talk through the options and read which way they are leaning. And keep going, until it is all sorted.

People come to me when it has all gone wrong, and they don't know how to fix things. That is why we are called Ninja HR, and why most of our work comes from other HR practitioners, CEOs and boards. I deal with the kind of HR situations that no-one else can fix.

Then I fix them.

Which is why I'm called **The Employment Genie.**

Whichever side I'm supporting (either the employer through Ninja HR, or the employee through the HR and Workers Trade Union), I ask people what they wish for. And then, assuming that what they have asked for doesn't break the laws of magic (even Genie's can't just do anything) then, well I make that happen!

But it is hard to explain in a few paragraphs. For now, here is a video of me explaining it (it is only three mins long)... and well, then you will just have to wait for my next book... Beyond HR, which I've already started. Then I will have the space and time to explain what it is I do differently.

Watch the video by scanning the QR code here ....

For now, you might just have to believe it is magic ☺.

So, if you want to learn how to solve impossible situations staffing situations in a way that seem to magically create solutions that staff and managers are happy with, then join the waiting list to find out how or get in touch if you need the help of the Employment Genie and **Ninja HR**.

Join the Beyond HR mailing list by scanning the QR code here ....

Chapter 15

The Entrepreneur Mindset Development Tool and The Sasspreneur Club

One day at ENC I had to support a small team of four to completely change. The powers that be had decided they wanted to scrap the team as it was and create something new. They wanted to keep the people and create four different jobs. So, I worked with the Head of Service, and we created a process to explain what would happen. The manager wasn't told ahead of schedule because they were one of the four.

We sat down in a conference room on one cold December morning a few weeks before Christmas. We had all the process and paperwork done, including explanations of the options for staff, and some draft job descriptions for the new roles.

By this point I'd done numerous of these types of events, including one in the NHS where I told 250 learning and development nurses that the intention was to seconde them to local government. My HR training and psychology and legal knowledge meant I knew how to structure a meeting and how to minimise the distress.

There were four people in that meeting and we got four completely different reactions.

When I'd been preparing for the meeting, I'd gone to the individual's files. One member of staff had a file that was four inches thick, full of grievances and annoyed letters. My heart sank. Most people don't have a thick file, and if they do, it means that they are probably not going to like what we do, whatever we do. So, I was I guess on high alert. But she was pleased. In her late fifties she smiled and asked whether voluntary redundancy was an option. It wasn't what we wanted, but it was an option that we had discussed and planned for. In local government a reorganisation like this in your late fifties triggers early retirement with protected pension status. She was pleased as punch. Well, that was easy.

The other three less so.

I bumped into number two in the corridor the day after.

"Hi, how are you feeling about yesterday, you OK?" I said.

"What do you mean, I didn't see you yesterday Aime".

Huh?

That really threw me. Doubting my own sanity I went and found the Trade Union rep that had been present.

"We did meet yesterday didn't we, to do the re-organisation meeting?"

Probably wondering if I'd lost the plot the Trade Union rep looked at me quizzically. We realised in the end that the whole meeting had been such a shock to number two that she had essentially blanked it from her memory. She had no recall that we even had the meeting, let alone what we had discussed. It was easier for her to deny it was happening than to deal with the reality of the fact that her job was changing. That was and is still the most extreme reaction to a change meeting I've ever experienced. And remember, we were talking about change, but we had said there would be four jobs for the four people and that their salaries would be protected. So, they weren't going to lose their jobs, the jobs were just going to change.

Number three was the team manager. He argued about everything for months. He basically questioned and challenged every line of the proposal and every suggestion we made. We wanted him to lead the new team, he was a good manager with great skills. But he fought everything we did, and nothing was good enough, and eventually after months, got another job at a different Council. To be honest in hindsight, I get it. This was something that was happening to him, and he had felt that he hadn't been involved (which he hadn't) so we had taken away his control. By changing his team we were also essentially saying it needed to change, which probably hit his ego pretty hard. I really felt for him...

Number four was a fabulous person, probably the strongest of the team, and we really wanted her to stay. But she just didn't want to talk to us about any of it. She said it was all too painful and she didn't want to talk about plans or proposals. She went off sick for a few days and then called in and just said she wanted to leave now without working her notice, and not talking to anyone, she just wanted to go. I felt sad, it had obviously hit her pretty hard.

We had done everything according to the book. We had tried to be kind, we had explained what was going on, we'd even followed every management piece of advice about how to handle change. But we'd still got four very different responses.

I thought a lot about this meeting and this process.

I read through some of the management and HR textbooks again, and Harvard Business Review articles and well pretty much anything I could get my hands on.

And I suddenly had an "aha moment" driving to work a few months later.

All the management guidance, all the HR procedural stuff. Most of the literature and guidance to managing the practical aspects of change in an organisation stem from Kotter's 8 stage change model[53] (or are similar to it).

1. Create urgency
2. Form a powerful coalition
3. Create a Vision for Change
4. Communicate the vision
5. Remove obstacles
6. Create Short term wins
7. Build on the change
8. Anchor the change in corporate culture

But what none of the HR or management literature seemed to

consider, was the individual. Without meaning to we had set up an experiment. We had brought four people with no prior knowledge of the change we were about to create into a room together. They all heard the same things, they all got the same paperwork, they all had the same outcome (their job was going to change, but they still had a job and their salaries would stay the same).

But they all reacted very differently.

Whether we had actually done the meeting well or not, one person was pleased, one found it so stressful they blocked it all out, one found it so stressful they didn't even want to talk about it and one wanted to argue about everything.

OK so then the variable had to be the people.

The different reactions, couldn't possibly have been created by our process (although they were sparked off or triggered by our process) the variation was the people.

Well this was interesting...

And well you may have worked out by now that, when I get an intellectual itch, when I go down a rabbit hole of investigation, I go deep.

So I did a bit more reading, and decided that this was a gap in the literature, so I looked around for experts and applied to De Montford University to do a PhD to study this.

I wanted to do the PhD across the psychology, HR and business management departments, but they wouldn't let me. But there was an expert in personality in the psychology department, and I had a psychology degree and a Masters, so I talked my way onto the psychology PhD programme. My working thesis title was "The impact of individual personality differences on organisational change".

I was doing it part time on top of my job, and it was great fun to be studying again. One of the things I liked best was going to talks from other PhD students about their research. A PhD programme is as much about learning to be an academic and learning how to write papers, submit papers to conferences, speak at conferences and teach undergraduates as it is your own research, and I loved every minute of it. Especially talking to students in different areas. I remember going to a presentation about some cutting edge technology in the physics department that was going to be able to potentially map the brain in a better way. Me being me I asked a few questions, and afterwards...

Mmm... do I tell these stories?

My good girl fears just popped into my head again. You see, I'm not brilliant at anything, I'm also not an expert at much, I am at heart a curious generalist. I know a little bit about a lot of things.

But I know that being honest about my brain upsets people. People think I'm boasting, or trying to make them feel small, or exaggerating, or at worst lying.

I'm a bright woman.

This bothers a lot of people.

I love to learn, and ask questions, and read and talk about stuff... so I keep learning.

But I'm telling these stories, because well they are just who I am. I'm enjoying sharing my experiences, it is fun to tell stories and share my life with you. But it also feels scary. Because if I share my life you might not like me. But I'm tired of pretending to be something that I'm not, if I hide, I'll probably be underestimated for my whole life, and not get the opportunities that would really excite me.

If I play small, then I will have to live small.

And I don't want to live small.

Ah yes, where were we? I was sitting in a lecture hall asking questions about a piece of physics tech.

Not many people asked questions, and afterwards the presenter and his tutor and colleagues literally climbed up the stairs into the auditorium to come and talk to me. As the audience filed out, they came and sat down around me and carried on the conversation that had started with my questions. I can't even remember exactly what the topic or the questions were, I just know that the question I had asked had clearly got to the heart of what they were trying to do.

"So what area physics are you studying for your PhD they asked"

"Urm... I'm not... the last time I did science was at GCSE, I'm doing"

They looked at me oddly, and the conversation kind of pettered out and got really embarrassing, so I made my excuses and ran off.

Why am I telling you this story?

Well it is just another example of a way I didn't fit in.

All the other PhD students were single minded in their areas of research, sometimes to an amazingly detailed way. Me, I was just enjoying surfing around the different topics and absorbing it all. I've never really ever found anyone who enjoys this or is drawn to it like I am, except maybe my Dad...

It had all felt so uncomfortable. So I stopped going to the other PhD events and just focused on my own area of research. It was hard going, because actually there wasn't much in this particular area. It is much easier to make generalisations, to try to come up with psychological theories that are supposedly true for everyone. When you start dealing with individuals then it gets more complicated. Or as my Dad would say (and he has a PhD in Educational Psychology, an undergraduate degree in teaching science, and a couple of masters, one in education and one in psychology) "don't try to work out how individual's are actually understanding things Aime, there are too many variables, that is impossible"...

Hmmm.

Challenge accepted.

So, I needed to find a way to identify individual differences but in a generalised way.

Well there are already lots of these in psychology they are called psychometric tests. You might have done Myers Briggs or DISC.

OK, so I needed to understand psychometric tests.

So I did the qualification to become a personality and occupational psychometric tester through the British Psychological Society. But that was a bit too basic for what I needed. What I really needed was to spend several days picking the brain of an expert.

So I bought some of the best books in the UK on psychometric tests and researched the authors. Found the best one and emailed him. He was retired and lived in Wales. Any chance I could pop down and pay you a one off fee to like pick your brains and learn about psychometric tests from the UK expert for a few days I asked?

He loved the idea, I booked an hotel and went to stay in Wales.

I also read everything I could find about the personality aspects of dealing with change.

But I didn't like the tone of some of the things I was reading.

Not only are there heavy criticisms of the validity of some of the common tests (it's all to do with bell curves, but is probably a bit techie for this book), but also, they seemed to presume one thing.

That personality was fixed.

That what was being tested was who you were, and that it wouldn't change, and then you were categorised in some way, or labelled.

Hmmm

But I'm not really the same every single day. Sometimes I'm very sociable, but when I'm struggling and the world feels too much, I tend to be very introverted. And I think that most people feel like this a little.

So, I decided I was going to create a mindset tool.

Not a psychometric test, because it wasn't going to try to find something that was fixed. It was going to ask where are you right now, not who are you.

Being an entrepreneur is basically dealing with a lot of change. So I took my academic research and adapted it to identify the seven mindsets entrepreneurs need. I intend to create a future version aimed at managers dealing with change

So armed with all this new knowledge I created the Entrepreneur Mindset Development Tool. I wrote all the questions and tested it with a small group of entrepreneurs. They loved it, in fact, I was a little overwhelmed by the response. They all wanted to talk about it more and find out how to grow in the areas I had identified.

Then the Kickstart Scheme and the HR and Workers Trade Union really picked up and I had to shelve my new product for eighteen months. As I started to wrap up the Kickstart Scheme I went back to the EMDT. I had already paid the fabulous Kelly Mayne to do some of the work to automate the tool but I'd run out of money.

I didn't want to borrow money, and going through a divorce and between businesses I didn't have any spare capital. I didn't want to seek external investors either.

Then I had a brainwave.

I obviously have a big thing about equal pay, but I realised that I didn't have to do things the way other people did.

So I decided I would be the change I wanted to see in the world and try to make things fairer.

And well you already know what happened next, Kelly Allen, Kelly Mayne and Clare McCabe came on board as my business partners. All with equal shares in the company.

When we started to write a bit about ourselves for our new website, I was a bit worried that it wouldn't seem equal. But Kelly M came up with a fabulous idea. She gave us names, and suggested we all answer the same set of questions. Kelly Allen is the organised one, Kelly Mayne is the techie one, Clare is the creative one and me, well she called me the original one 😂.

We set about getting the tool automated and ready to go.

My initial concern was that I didn't have the capacity to coach and support people who did the tool. I was worried that someone might do the tool in the middle of the night after being made redundant and get scores and think that they weren't good enough, I wanted them to do the tool in a supportive environment.

If I'm honest, I was also a little burnt out, I wasn't sure I could do much more, and I thought that if I could sell via coaches then not only could they help me design what clients needed, but also they could then offer the support (and I wouldn't need to).

So, on a sunny day in London in June 2023, I put out a call on social media asking for curious coaches. My target was to sell to six coaches in the initial cohort, and give them lifetime accreditation, and then they could use the EMDT with their clients and work out what kind of support clients found useful. Now I had a clear idea of what I thought would work, but I was hoping to get some really experienced coaches who would give me ideas. It was an unusual moment of imposter syndrome for me.

I hoped I could sell the first cohort within the first three months. I sold out in the first two weeks. And wow, I had some of the most amazing coaches you could possibly imagine join up, including Sandra Whiles, Katy Walton and Dee Beckett.

We had the first session, and it went horribly wrong.

I expected them to give me lots of feedback about how they would use the tool. They actually said they needed more from me. They kindly reminded me that I had been thinking about this for years, and that these were new concepts to them, and they needed more support and guidance from me. That was not what I was expecting. And I had an even bigger imposter syndrome moment.

But then I put on my big girl pants. OK Aime, these are wonderful people that trust you, and they are saying that they think you have more to give, and they need that.

It took me about a month to get my head around what was needed… but I came up with a plan and sent it out, and then met up with all of them on zoom.

I was shit scared. What if I had completely misjudged what they needed?

But they loved it, and the EMDT Coaches Accreditation

Programme was born. It includes twelve action learning sessions with me, talking about twelve different topics, following a video from me sent out two weeks before each session. The programme lasts fourteen months, includes a test at the end (to check they understand the content) and then a completion party face-to-face to hand out the very first EMDT Coaches Accreditation Programme Certificates.

They were even pleased that I was going to test them!

You might at this point be wondering what the seven mindsets that the tool identifies are, that my research identified as being vital to manage change and be a great entrepreneur. They are:

- Locus of Control
- Risk tolerance
- Ambiguity tolerance
- Optimism
- Curiosity
- Self Efficacy
- Growth Mindset

As part of the social media marketing to get the first cohort of coaches I had put out some videos explaining these mindsets and then something unexpected happened.

People kept asking me if they could do the EMDT without having a coach. Because it had been coded then and Kelly had given me a special free link straight to the online tool on my phone, I talked various people through it, and they did it then and there on my phone. The scores came up automatically and I explained them. I watched their faces and they all seemed to love doing it, and it tended to result in dozens of questions and lots of discussion. And as people started to hear about it they wanted to do it directly as well. And the cohort one said that they needed more explanation readily available to their clients from me, that they could then add to about what the tool was, and what these mindsets are, and why they matter, and of course most importantly what people can do to increase their scores.

Now, I have always strongly argued that it isn't always just about getting a high score, and extreme highs are not necessarily great (extreme risk tolerance is likely to suggest a gambler and risk taker, and extreme locus of control makes it hard for people to let go and realise that some things are out of their control). But I realised, that part of the reason I hadn't created this, was just that I was tired... it has been a tough few years.

But well, things were getting easier. So, I've created a standalone EMDT package including training and guidance, and a report, as well as the opportunity to do the tool. I still think it will be better to do it with a coach, but if you fancy finding out more, you can buy this package at a special rate as you've bought this book and got this far! For a short time only, it will be £19 to take the test and get the report and support package. And well if you would like to find a coach to support you more in your mindset work, then we can recommend some excellent coaches!

So don't wait, if you want to find out more about EMDT, whether you have the mindset to be an entrepreneur, or want to learn how to have a more entrepreneurial mindset without necessarily needing to spend thousands of pounds on a coach, then why not have a look?

Find out your current Entrepreneurial Mindset scores now by scanning the QR code here ....

And the **Sasspreneur Club**, well that is what we are calling ourselves. We haven't worked out everything that we might offer beyond the EMDT initial package and the EMDT Coaches Accreditation Programme, but I have lots of ideas, and it is going to be fun trying them out and seeing what you think. I'm also looking forward to collaborating with lots of the amazing entrepreneurs that I now consider friends. Because this isn't about competition, this is about doing things together, and all learning together.

It is going to be such fun!

Join the Sasspreneur Club mailing list by scanning the QR code here ....

Chapter 16
DIY HR for small businesses

It's tough working in HR. HR professionals are expected to deal with a lot, not only all the procedures and law, but also help advise organisations and individuals in some incredibly difficult situations.

Over my career I have had to call the police twice (once because a gunman had a loaded gun pointed at a manager's head in the basement of Tower 42, once because a member of staff's husband was currently knocking down her brother's door with an axe to kill him - both of those make excellent stories if you ever get me alone in a bar with a bit of spare time and a drink or two).

I've also dealt with fraud, sexual abuse, bullying, actual deaths (both at work and due to ill health), and well I'll stop there. I once told a story about fifteen dead guinea pigs and realised that the story was far too dark for the audience and well whoops...

Having worked in the NHS and Local Government, including sitting on the clinical governance board in a mental Health Trust and working in Social Services, Education and Housing, lets just say I have seen more than most people.

But even without working in those settings, HR frequently have to deal with employees who are the end of their tether, or who have had terrible things happen to them. Whether that is rape, issues to do with family members, ill health, financial issues.

And well it didn't get easier when I started up a Trade Union of last resort...

So the burnout rates following Covid in HR roles are very high. Higher than they have ever been. The expectations that we can help recruit to any job, create an amazing culture, engage with staff despite the behaviour of the board, despite the actual culture, despite the assumptions and behaviours around is.. Well it is just impossible most of the time.

So HR professionals are leaving in droves. And one of the current things many do, is set up their own HR consultancy and seek to help small businesses and charities with their HR.

That is exactly what I did.

Because well small businesses don't have HR departments so they must need us right?

Wrong.

HR as a function, and the way most of us were trained and learnt, is essentially a function that is designed for large organisations. Small ones at best have a standalone HR person, but that requires one person to take on every specialism. It is like a GP trying to be a heart surgeon, a paediatrician, a psychiatrist, a cancer specialist all in one with no referral to others. GPs are AMAZING, but they do refer to specialists when they get to the limit of their knowledge, they don't get you on the table and start to perform open heart surgery there and then. And I'm glad they don't, because they can't be a specialist in every area.

But in HR there is often the expectation that a single HR professional CAN do be an expert in recruitment, and employee relations and learning and development and benefits and payroll and mediation.

Most HR professionals also have not learnt much about marketing or sales or product development or operations or all the other types of knowledge and skills needed to run a small business.

And one of the biggest things I've learnt on my entrepreneurial journey over the last five years is that it is important to understand what it is that the customer needs. What is the problem they are trying to solve?

Not the problem I think they should solve.

Not the thing I think is their problem.

But what is their actual problem?

Most sales boil down to two very basic human reactions.

Moving away from something unpleasant.

Moving toward something pleasant.

And in a small business, even a medium sized business, keeping afloat is a daily issue. You don't spend money on things that aren't a problem today.

But HR basically works on the model of putting a lot of time and effort into policies and procedures to try and avoid problems later. But most people don't read the policies and they don't necessarily avoid the problem either.

Did you know it isn't a legal requirement to have HR policies?

But small businesses do have issues around staffing. And they do get into difficulties managing things like maternity or grievances or long term ill health.

There are basically three strategies small/medium sized businesses take to deal with HR until they hit about 50 to a hundred staff (when they usually take on someone to be their HR lead, or give someone the role even if they aren't qualified - it's always amused me that HR and Facilities or office manager are often merged even though they are totally different professions and skill sets - I mean why not merge cleaner and sales director or finance manager and receptionist).

1. Sign up to one of the big companies.
2. Wing it.
3. Hire an independent HR consultant.

But all of these strategies can be very expensive in their own way.

So I've been redesigning an approach for small businesses and testing it in practice. It has been an absolute blast! I do tend to do things very differently, that is one of the benefits of having lots of experience, you can then start to be creative. I remember one client who simply thought what I was suggesting was impossible, but he was in a really tight fix, so thought it wouldn't hurt if he let me have a go. He was incredibly surprised when I pulled it off. The look on his face was what gave me the idea to call myself The Employment Genie. You see anything can look like a bit of magic if it is not what you expected. What I've created, I call it

DIY HR for small businesses. It is very different, and it is still under wraps for now. It takes a totally different approach to dealing with staffing issues, and makes it accessible to any small business owner without becoming an expert in HR or employment law, and without needing lots of policies and procedures, or even hiring an HR person.

If you are interested in finding out more, and being first to hear about new products and training to allow you to DIY your HR, then follow the QR code to sign up now. Who knows you might get the opportunity to trial out something new and get something for free while we are still testing things!

Join the DIY HR mailing list by scanning the QR code here ....

Chapter 17
The Niche Awards

I kind of vaguely knew that there were business awards around, but I'd only been in business a couple of years in 2021, and to be honest I was busy just trying to keep my head above water, so I hadn't really given them much thought.

Then I got some emails saying that I had been nominated for four different Niche Awards.

I nearly fell off my chair.

I was nominated for Small Business of the Year, Professional Services Company of the Year, Entrepreneur of the Year and Female Entrepreneur of the Year.

I rang my business coach Dee Beckett to let her know and find out what the hell I had to do next, and then the penny dropped. She had nominated me.

I was really touched. She knew me and my business inside and out.

And she had taken the trouble, in her own time, without asking me, to fill out the forms to nominate me.

I grinned for 24 hours.

Then I had to submit some more paperwork which I did, but Dee suggested that I got a video done. Really? Me on a video? That sounded a bit far fetched and to be honest, way out of my league as a start up. Plus you know, me on video.

I guess I need to go back a little bit. I used to hate having my photo taken. Its a real shame but there really aren't many photos of me between about 18 and 40, not even with my kids. I just saw myself as ugly and fat and incredibly un-photogenic.

But through networking I had met Katy Wheatley and Matt Glover.

Katy is an amazing women and I'd count her now as a great friend, and her life has morphed several times, but back then she was running a business selling vintage clothes and helping people like me to find their styles. She recommended that I look up a designer called Kemi Telford, and well the rest is history. If you've ever seen me on social media in a colourful skirt, it is very very likely it is a Kemi Telford original, I have seven. And Matt said that he could take great pictures of me (he's a brand photographer, as well as currently writing an amazing cookbook).

Yeah right...

They ganged up on me, and all three of us went into Leicester.

It didn't start well. I was trying to make sense of everything that Matt was telling me to do and my brain just overloaded. I was trying to remember it all and do it all and it just wasn't working. As I may have mentioned before, I can't act. I need to actually be in the mood I want to portray, and grumpy, confused, scared, ugly feeling Aime wasn't a great look. Katy suggested we stop and eat chips and cake. A very good idea, and Matt took a hilarious photo of me with my head in my hands. After some refreshment we went outside to try something different. The sun was shining, and full of chips and cake I was in a better mood. Matt was trying to get me to pose in front of a door next to the Cathedral when a really handsome, incredibly smartly dressed man came up to me and started chatting.

These things happen to me a lot, anyone that knows me knows that I'm a magnet for the unusual, and well I kind of love it. It must be something about energy levels or resonance or pheromones or something, all I know is people seem drawn to me and want to tell me their life stories, whether I'm on a bus, train or well in the street. He didn't want to stop talking to me, but he was making like zero sense, and it was all very odd because well at this point Matt was kinda trying to climb up the side of the cathedral to get a good angle. Then the smartly dressed bloke lay down on the floor in a puddle and tried to start swimming. The puddle was about an inch deep and no more than a foot long, but he was lying on his front miming full legs and arms front crawl.

The three of us just burst into laughter. It was just the strangest five minutes, and seeing him lying there in his very expensive tweed three-piece suit happily trying to swim in his puddle was just bizarre (he seemed a very happy, if he'd been upset or ill we would of course stepped in and tried to get him to safety).

Matt seized the moment and the change in energy and I started prancing around with Katy climbing walls, throwing my hair about, and generally just laughing and being silly (thinking back I might have had a Gin and Tonic or two with those chips). And I completely forgot that anyone was taking photos.

I was astonished when the photos came back. They were me, but well they weren't me. They were somehow a better version of me.

For the first time in my life, I realised that it was actually possible for a lovely photo of me to exist.

This was a massive realisation.

Massive.

Because believing something is possible is often all it takes to believe you can do it again.

And now, well if you see my beaming face all over social media, it is because I've done loads of sessions with Matt and he's taught me lots, including how to take a selfie. And well that first session just totally changed my confidence about having my photo taken (so thank you Matt and Katy - you are both legends!).

So back to the Niche awards, well if I was going to have a video taken, I knew that Matt had started working with a really amazing new videographer, who was really young but amazingly talented. They hadn't worked together much then, so I got a steal of a deal and they agreed to do me a short video to submit with the paperwork for the Niche awards.

I wasn't an ideal client. I can't learn lines and say them naturally. So instead I just talked off the cuff, and let them video for an hour while we wandered round Leicester, and then hoped to hell they might be able cut it together to make something useful.

Watch the video by scanning the QR code here ....

There were several rounds to the Niche awards, a semi final then a final. And to my utter amazement I went through to the final of the Professional Services Company of the Year. This category includes legal firms, accountants, tax professionals and lots of other HR and training companies. I booked a table for the Ninja HR team, and invited my Mum and sister and friends and decided that we would just have a great night out. I didn't expect to win, hell I was amazed I'd got this far, but I do like a party!

Matt came just before we went in and took some of my favourite shots of us as a team, there is one of them on the front of this book! And a lovely shot of me drinking champagne in the sunshine (we hadn't even gone in yet).

The Niche awards is a big night in Leicester. It is held in the Athena which is an old 1930s cinema that has been converted into a venue. It holds 500 odd people and was packed full of people in black tie drinking and eating. I got steadily drunker, and then it got to the point where they read out the winners of the Professional Services Category.

I won.

I was so shocked I just sat in silence. My sister had been videoing, but stopped because she hadn't heard the outcome and assumed from my face I'd lost. After everything that had happened I'm not sure what was more difficult, the thought of losing or of winning.

But I had won. In my second year, against amazing competition, after everything that had happened, me and the Ninja HR team had won professional services company of the year.

Milly, my fabulous friend and my Chief Operating Officer for the Kickstart Scheme grabbed my arm. Fuck I was going to have to go up on stage and give a speech.

Mercifully the sound system wasn't working great, so the garbled rubbish that came out of my mouth was heard by few, and note to self, do not run across a stage in a posh dress no matter how excited you are, you might actually knock someone out with your boobs and it looks like a porno on video (and yes I have that video, but I'm not sharing it!).

So I had won.

But my journey with the Niche Awards didn't end there. I was invited by the fabulous Jenny Cross (owner and CEO of Cross Productions that runs the Niche awards) to be a Judge the following year.

And well the year after I became Head Judge.

I'm now in charge of designing and creating the judging criteria, helping to create the judging timetable and process, and of course sitting on the panels to interview the finalists. Oh, and dealing with any problems (there aren't many but people do have some strong opinions).

Because one of the things that people assume is that Jenny decides who wins. But she doesn't, she is completely separate from the judging team. In fact, so is the whole Cross Productions team. Jenny knew when she appointed me that I would do what was right and wouldn't even let her hassle me. The exact opposite of brown paper envelopes at dawn.

And I created a fair and open judging criteria that takes everything that the Niche awards stands for and highlights it. We look for the unusual, the creative, the people who have crafted businesses from nothing, and who give amazing customer service. Many business awards hand out to the prizes to the biggest and the best, and of course we do look at growth and financial figures, but we also give a score for "scrappiness".

It is always a pleasure to meet all the amazing finalists. And often I'm left with tears in my eyes after hearing their amazing stories... Judging the community impact and charity of the year awards are especially challenging. But this is power, soft power, but power all the same. There is only one way to win, and that is to be awesome, but you do have to enter. This year I'm hoping that more female led companies enter, and you can nominate yourselves (in fact most of the male led companies do just that). I can't guarantee you will win, but put yourselves out there, and you never know, you might surprise yourself... it certainly surprised me.

And whilst I don't get paid for being the Head Judge (I have a very simple rule, I don't take money to recommend anyone or anything or for things like this - that way there can be no hint of collusion). I have been asked to recommend things for money, which made my kids howl (mum there is no way you are actually an influencer), but well, who said middle aged mums can't be influencers... I just choose slightly different path...

And in 2024 I am also part of the judging team for the entrepreneur's entrepreneur award category at the Real Entrepreneur Awards.

I still have to pinch myself.

So, after all that horribleness at ENC I have set up a Trade Union and supported more than 50 members through some of the most difficult experiences of their life. I have set up an HR consultancy firm (Ninja HR). I have scaled a Kickstart Gateway to create 237 Kickstart job placement for unemployed young people in a pandemic. I have created a new mindset development tool that stemmed from my PhD studies, built a team and an automated website to deliver the EMDT. Oh, and I've created two new ways of doing HR, Beyond HR for larger companies and DIY for Smaller Companies, and won a Niche Award, become Head Judge, got divorced, found myself, and made lots of friends.

Not bad really.

And well, I'm not done yet...

In fact, it kind of feels like I'm just getting started...

PART FIVE:
The final word

Chapter 18
The Final Battle?

Well, my story is nearing its end. Thank you so much for reading this far, it means a lot to me, it really does. I read once that the desire to write can often come from the feeling of not being heard, and for me I definitely feel there is some truth to that, and this process has definitely been incredibly cathartic for me.

This chapter is a little bit about the final Employment Tribunal case, but it is also about our legal system, and about how not to deal with difficult women at work.

Our legal system is inherently adversarial.

The logic is that a good fight will bring out the truth, and to be fair sometimes it can.

But rarely.

Going to court is expensive, time consuming, exhausting and scary. Winning is as much about who can afford the biggest and best legal team as it is about justice. It is one of the reasons we used to have legal aid (so everyone could afford a lawyer) but that has all but disappeared, biasing the system heavily on the side of the wealthy.

A standard tactic of the rich and powerful is to out lawyer everyone else, and bury the little person with paperwork and bureaucracy for good measure, hoping that they will give up long before they get to court.

But it has always been possible to defend yourself in court.

No matter how big, rich and powerful your opposition, you always have the opportunity to fight your own corner. A David and Goliath fight yes, and one that almost every David loses.

But sometimes it is the principle that matters.

And for me, this was never about winning, it was about standing up and saying this is not OK, no matter what you throw at me, no matter how hard it is, it is still not OK.

It took so long to get to court, more than three years, (delay tactics are used commonly, plus the courts are backed up) that by the time we finally got to the Employment Tribunal East Northamptonshire Council didn't exist. It had been dissolved and replaced by a new Council. My case was passed over to North Northamptonshire Council as a legacy matter.

Apparently Glenn Hammons hadn't told the new bosses about the ongoing legal case with me. This should have been handed over as a potential financial risk, and the new organisation were apparently furious. Especially as they had recently had to settle another case leftover from ENC for £4 million.

The Leader of the Council took an unusual step of sending out an email about my case to all councillors. One of which shared it with the press[54]. The memo described the case as a financial "high risk" for the authority, which is apparently why all Councillors were informed.

The email also said "I believe that is essential that I am not only aware of, but that I communicate on, those legal cases that are deemed to be "high risk matters" such as Monks, and in line with that I have been made aware of an employment matter..."

Whilst it was quite a shock to find that the Council had leaked highly sensitive and personal information to the press, it was on some level satisfying that they had felt that it was a high risk financially matter enough to send an email to all the elected councillors… and it did lead to the rather surreal situation of being contacted by the Telegraph and having the issue raised in Private Eye…

Kate Cronin, the journalist for the Northamptonshire Telegraph telephoned me a couple of times having found my details on the internet through my business. To be fair she was incredibly supportive, but I just wasn't ready to tell my tale and I was scared that if I spoke out before the tribunal it might jeopardise my case in some way.

Clearly worried, North Northamptonshire Council appointed a top legal team. I defended myself. Realistically the only option as it would have cost me about £150,000 to employ a legal team to take on the case. There were two pre-trial hearings, and the final hearing lasted ten days, with a hearing bundle that was 3,007 pages long.

Low level intimidation and strategic confuddlement is a standard tactic when a team of lawyers are up against someone defending themselves. Halfway through the second pre-trial hearing, ten minutes before the lunch break was over, the barrister defending NNC presented me with a ten side submission to ask for interim costs of £5,000 payable immediately.

He pretended to be all friendly and said something along the lines of

"Look I don't have a choice about submitting this, but I should warn you that you will probably lose this action and have to pay £5,000 now to progress, unless of course you want to settle now. Would you like me to ask the Judge to delay the rest of this hearing while we negotiate. I think I can still persuade them to offer you at least £30,000 possibly much more, and then you can go home and you won't have to deal with this anymore".

He told it as syrupy as you like as if he was my best friend and then showed me a photo of his pet donkeys (I mean seriously you can't make this shit up – Donkeys?).

One of the things you do when you are representing yourself is do lots of preparation. I'm not a lawyer, and I didn't have a team to research for me. So, getting this kind of thing five minutes before going into court is really difficult to deal with.

But of course, that is why they do it. It is meant to befuddle and confuse and panic.

To be fair it nearly worked. I was exhausted. I had run out of steam, and it was taking everything I had to try and understand the complex legal procedural rules and social expectations. But this was never about the money, and I knew what they were doing was trying to trip me up, but what I didn't know was whether it would work.

I decided to stand my ground and take the risk.

We went back in, and the barrister presented it to the Judge. I asked for time to prepare a defence and the Judge said no, he would hear arguments now.

Oh fuck.

How the hell was I going to defend myself on this matter with no preparation time?

Well OK then, no choice I guess, so I did the best I could.

The Judge then threw the submission out and ruled that there was a reasonable chance of success in the case therefore it wasn't appropriate to ask for any up front costs.

Generally costs aren't payable in Employment Tribunal matters (unlike in other courts) but very occasionally they are awarded.

I left literally shaking. I didn't have to pay costs, and well I now knew at least I had a reasonable case. Nice to know.... I lived to fight another day.

I went back to my airbnb and collapsed onto the bed, I didn't even have the energy to eat (and anyone who knows me knows things have to be very very bad for me to lose my apetite!).

Preparing the bundle was overwhelming, they sent three versions over two weeks, leaving everything to the last minute. I needed to check 3,007 pages, three times, look for things they had added that I hadn't ever seen before (they had buried some interesting nuggets) and check they hadn't "accidentally" missed out anything that I had requested should be included. Again, another strategy, bury the employee who is defending themselves in paperwork and hope they don't find the legal nuggets, and ideally, they give up...

They had a team to look through the paperwork.

Against little old me, on my own.

It's a good job I read fast!

Keep going Aime, I kept telling myself, just keep going, one step at a time, you've got this.

I felt almost ready to do this thing, then the court changed from Cambridge to Norwich at the last minute, just after the deadline for my refund of my airbnb... deep breaths Aime just book somewhere else.

But even in the darkest times, sometimes you get a bit of luck. I apparently have a really high AirBNB user score, mainly I guess because I don't leave the place in a mess. So I managed to book this beautiful converted flat in the attic of a listed building. It was my home from home for two weeks and felt safe and lovely. I was the first ever guest and the host was simply lovely, he even took me out for drink or two, and asked me each day how I was, and his lovely little dog always seemed to manage to sneak up the stairs and push through my door and climb onto my bed.

I may have been completely alone, I may have been doing the most difficult thing emotionally and intellectually in my whole life, but the universe had sent me some warmth and friendship at a time when I needed it.

To be fair various people had offered to come with me to support me, but I'd said no. I knew that I would end up spending all my time trying to explain the legalities of what was going on, or the tactics or dealing with their emotions. Not for the first time in my life, but maybe the last, I decided it would be easier to just be on my own.

When I moved back in with my parents after getting divorced, exhausted and needing somewhere warm and safe, I still didn't let my mum and dad do anything for me. I am a very independent person, and I don't like people helping me. I read somewhere that extreme independence is a trust issue, and I realised that I wasn't letting anyone in. I had no real reason not to trust people (or not that I can remember) but I never have. My mum, frustrated at me avoiding any help, already feeling hugely embarrassed about going home and being in the way, finally blurted out "you have always been impossible to help Aime, ever since you were a small child, will you please just let us help you?". Blimey, fair point, well made, OK then.

I've been living with my folks for more than a year, and it has been surprisingly great, especially when I finally realised that they seemed to actually quite like having me around, and missed me when I went off to London, or Leicester or Devon as I often do. And well, I got better at letting them look after me. I still don't let Mum do my washing (although she still surreptitiously tries to sometimes) but I do let them cook for me. To be honest if I ever move out, I shall miss pancakes for breakfast on Sundays, and Mum making my favourite dinners, and always making sure the fridge is stocked with all my favourite foods. And I love having long conversations with my Dad about books we are reading, education, politics, science, economics.... It occurs to me that not everyone gets to spend quality time with their folks as they get older, and I'm lucky that I can. And well at least I empty the dishwasher, and sometimes drop them off at their friends' houses and then pick them up so they can drink far too much... which they love...

So yes, letting anyone help me, is a struggle, just ask my siblings, or my good friend Clare, in fact any of my friends. But I'm getting better... honest...

So back to my story. Where were we, ah yes, I had arrived in Norwich, and dragged three suitcases (one of clothes, one of legal books and one of legal papers) up narrow stairs ready for ten days in court.

I knew it was going to be close. I had heard the barrister arguing with the appointing solicitor. They were arguing so loudly I could hear everything they said, and they were very worried that they would lose.

We had also tried judicial mediation. The Judge undertaking the mediation confirmed that there was potentially a winnable case, and recommended that we settle and save the courts the cost of hearing the case (10 days probably costed the Court system at least £100,000). He calculated that the cost to defend the case from that point onwards was between £70,00 and £130,000 for North Northamptonshire Council.

Employers don't get costs back even if they win, so he suggested they settle for a figure that was less than the legal fees they would have to pay. But they wouldn't settle without me agreeing to being silenced. The judge said that was not right and got fed up with them. He ended the judicial mediation early, annoyed, saying that they hadn't really been prepared to negotiate, and that the mediation had been a waste of time.

It would have been nice to settle, but I wasn't prepared to sign a gag clause, that would have left a horrible taste in my mouth for the rest of my life. I'm hugely reflective and supportive of people that do sign them, and I help plenty of Trade Union clients and Ninja HR clients sign settlement agreements, but I don't believe in Non Disclosure Clauses.

The case didn't start well. The lead Judge (there are three in a complex employment tribunal) asked opposing counsel (the other side's barrister) if he minded if we finished early on Friday. They discussed the options, and agreed it was OK. He never even looked in my direction or asked my opinion. It was just up to him and the barrister, I was clearly irrelevant. This is extremely poor legal practice and quite frankly rude, and it didn't bode well for my chances.

The court case was both one of the most harrowing, and exhilarating experiences of my life. I won many legal and practical points, and I survived two and a half days being cross examined by counsel. He asked me three times, whether "I had asked for it?". He was intentionally using such loaded and provocative language to try and unsettle and upset me. It didn't work.

Basically his legal argument was that David Oliver and Glenn Hammons were entitled to do everything they had done, because I had asked for it. Because I was difficult. Because I was a trouble maker.

I even cross examined the current Conservative candidate for the Wellingborough by-election Helen Harrison. She did not like being questioned by me. She had been the Chair of the Committee that had decided that David Oliver's behaviour was perfectly acceptable, and also the Chair of the Committee that decided on my Equal Pay Grievance. She got rattled and defensive when I questioned her. When I asked her a technical question about her understanding of the job evaluation scheme, one that she should have been able to answer by the way, she snapped at me and said

"I can't be expected to know that, I'm just a physiotherapist. I don't know how Job Evaluation and Equal Pay works, I just went with what the experts and the officers and other councillor's had decided".

In my opinion, having worked with Helen Harrison, and seen how she thinks and what she knows, I do not believe she has the skills, knowledge or aptitude to be a an effective MP, although of course she may still get elected...

I collapsed at the end of the case, and found out in an email months and months later that I had lost my case.

The Employment Tribunal had decided that East Northamptonshire Council was entitled to treat me the way they had.

But did I really lose?

It was never about winning in court (although that would have been nice). It was about becoming a free woman. It was about letting go of that social conditioning that had made me a good girl. It was about being prepared to do whatever it took to say, I know what happened and what happened wasn't OK, whatever the court felt.

And, well I did give them a good run for their money.

And I did learn lots.

Including how to fight a complicated employment tribunal.

And I did get lots of court experience.

And I did prove to myself, that I am incredibly resilient.

And I did have the satisfaction of the investigation reports that said that David Oliver had treated me badly, and that raising my whistleblowing allegations was fair, and that pay was not equal. Even if the Judges at the employment tribunal had decided that they were allowed to do everything that they did.

I could have appealed, but it was time to stop.

And well I never did sign that non-disclosure agreement, so I could do the one thing that so few people in this situation can ever do (almost everyone settles) I could tell my story.

And use that story and experience to help other people.

So, whilst technically I didn't win.

I'm taking it as a different type of win.

One of the mindsets in the EMDT is the growth mindset. It is about how you frame a mistake or a failure. Does it mean you are rubbish? Or does it mean that you didn't get it right this time, but maybe you will next time? And maybe you might have learnt something? And maybe you can be good enough even if no one believes you...

So, through all of this, I had not only become a free woman, I had also helped developed my entrepreneurial mindsets. In fact, I had massively increased my scores on four of the mindsets since I had left ENC (Growth Mindset, Risk Tolerance, Ambiguity Tolerance and Self Efficacy). It isn't about always winning, it is, as Roosevelt said, about being prepared to enter the ring...

But did ENC win?

And was there another way?

Personally, I don't think they won either, but let me explain...

Being an HR professional who has found her niche in managing the most extreme of cases, and trying to use everything I know, from employment law and design to emotional intelligence and psychology, it has occurred to me to ask the following question.

What would I have advised David Oliver, East Northamptonshire Council and North Northamptonshire Council to do if they had had to handle a situation and a person like me?

I would have considered what did the organisation want and what did the employee want, and tried to find an overlap and a way of finding a solution that recognised the needs, expectations and understanding of truth and reality that worked for all parties? It is essentially a creative process that weaves together many different types of knowledge to create something that is a collaborative project in essence, a moving together of understanding and truth. It isn't easy to do, and is why I call myself The Employment Genie, because it can seem to be a bit like magic when it works well...

The organisational and management perspectives are usually fairly easy to gauge. Most organisations and managers want to find a resolution to the conflict with as little hassle, financial outlay, and risk as possible. Almost all managers also want to find a solution that keeps their ego intact. They want to feel that they did the right thing, that they didn't mess things up and that they were great. We all have an ego and it needs massaging probably more than we care to admit.

A very small number of managers comprehend that the organisation in the medium and long term will benefit from an added layer, that of learning what went wrong, what could we do differently next time? What can we learn about our employees, our customers and our world from this situation? But to do that, they may have to accept that they need to see and hear more than is comfortable for their own ego. They may need to notice mistakes and things that could have been done better. The organisations that have leaders that can do this will thrive, as they can weather and flourish and adapt in a VUCA world.

Usually, understanding the employee and what they are emotionally upset by is the way to achieve the best outcome for the organisation and managers. Because if we can understand then we can design a process and a solution that meets those needs and de-escalates the problem. But it requires a desire and a capability to try to understand, and the resilience to cope with what they might hear. It requires genuine empathy and compassion, which are rare in senior management.

We live in a world where we are emotionally bombarded with pain and distress and lust and love and for most of us most of the time it is too much, we need to screen it out, ignore it, move on, or we would not get through the day. But it is hard to hear someone, someone you need and want to hear when you have already reached your capacity for empathy that day, week, month, year, lifetime. And that leads to burnout. But fundamentally it is reaching a point of emotional overwhelm, where our limited human souls can take no more, and the only solution is to shut down to try to process and heal from that which we have already been exposed to. The world is essentially an overwhelmingly emotional place full of triggers, often intentionally placed there to grab our attention in an already loud environment. For those with any type of neurodiversity it is doubly, maybe tenfold, as overwhelming.

But understanding is the only way through.

So back to how I would have dealt with me.

What did I want?

Emotionally there were fundamentally three things I wanted, and these are common:

1. I wanted to be heard, if I had concerns and worries, I wanted them to be heard with kindness and understanding. I wanted those feelings to be acknowledged.

2. I wanted to be recognised. I am a professional, knowledgeable and capable women, and I wanted to feel that expertise and my value had been noticed and was appreciated.

3. I wanted to be accepted. I wanted to feel I was part of the team, I wanted to feel I had a role and I could be useful.

It seems so obvious when it is written out like that doesn't it, yet it is incredibly difficult to do this on a day-by-day basis, and it takes time to learn the skills and the emotional resilience to do this. We all have to make choices in our lives and sacrifice one thing for another, there are always opportunity costs. If you are feeling "fucking hell this Aime person knows a lot, she seems to know more than me, is she better than me?" Remember that I have sacrificed other things to gain this knowledge. My marriage fell apart, I did not spend as long with my children growing up as I'd have liked to, I do not focus on my physical health, and I can't ice skate or do my own hair or makeup. I am not better than you, I have just chosen to spend my time differently. And to be fair, chosen is the wrong word, I felt compelled by different things than you that is all.

But together that is where the real magic is.

I was incredibly lucky that my girls went to nurseries where they were cared for and loved, they played in the sunshine and climbed into buckets, and the incredibly skilled and fabulous team that ran the place were genuinely delighted by every painting that they ever painted, and created different opportunities for them to play every day.

I can do that a little bit, but I get bored, I'm much better with my girls now they are adults, and fortunately for me they only appear to hate me a small (and healthy) proportion of the time, and well quite frankly they will hopefully be adults for 70 plus years.

OK, so back to how to handle Aime (or any other employee). Once you've worked out what they need emotionally, and what you and the organisation need both emotionally and practically (and yes managers are all human, for now at least, so yes they all have emotions even if they don't acknowledge them) then you can design a solution that meets everyone's needs.

For me, a great manager that had made me feel heard recognised and accepted from the start would have found they would have got my undying loyalty and commitment from the very beginning. If they had also realised that I am inherently curious and like to solve complex problems, they could have leveraged my needs and the organisations needs (as I'm fundamentally not that interested in power or money or status) and I'd have happily been a little engine of usefulness. But to be fair, there aren't many managers out there like that, so most of the time we need to create a solution to a problem that has already got quite serious. So, let's go back to this story at the moment when I put in those three emails, when I'm clearly upset. So, if David had invited me out for lunch, and basically said the following, my anger and upset would have dissipated.

"Aime, I am incredibly sorry that I have upset you. I had absolutely no intention of making you feel this way, and truly wish that I hadn't. I can tell that you feel hurt and that you have concerns. I hope that we haven't got an equal pay issue, but we may have. I want this organisation to pay everyone fairly and I think you can help us do this. Can you help me work through what we do? We will look at all your concerns, and review how decisions are made with an open mind, and if we find anything that is not quite right, we will fix it. I don't think I've earnt your trust and respect yet, but I'd like to, and I'd like you to work on a few projects with me. I would value your input and thoughts; you are clearly a bright and capable woman and I think you have so much to offer. I don't have all the answers, but together with the other fabulous members of the team, we can achieve so much. Will you give me a second chance, and together we can really help create an amazing organisation that supports staff and delivers amazing things with the community?".

If he had said all of that, I would have walked away with a grin on my face, completely forgiving him, and feeling all warm and fuzzy and excited.

So easy, and yet so hard. And so easy in hindsight...

I don't believe that David Oliver or Glenn Hammons had the leadership capability to deal with me on a good day, let alone me when I was upset or angry, and I have some sympathy for that. But others have managed, and either they needed to become better leaders, or step aside so others could be better leaders. We have had too much poor leadership in our public sector organisations for too long, and we all suffer the consequences.

There is another stage by the way to resolving this situation, after the speech above, and that is to follow through and do all of those things and continue to notice how an employee is feeling (which is hard). Some people have learnt to say all of the above in the moment, but don't mean it and don't carry through. That is disastrous and is likely to blow up even worse than not saying it all.

As Council's have a requirement for transparency in their budgets, I trawled through the records to try to calculate (I had to use a bit of estimation as not all the data was available) how much ENC and NNC had spent "fighting me in court" and the estimated figures look like this...

Legal fees.....	£183,321
External investigation and consultancy fees......	£63,284
Time of managers and staff taken up in 23 hearings	£84,682
Total..................	**£331,287**

(and this doesn't include the court costs which were probably at least another £100,000)

Currently Council Tax Band D at North Northamptonshire Council is £2,188.50 per year.

So, if I divide the total spent it means that 151 households paid their full Council Tax merely to fight me.

Or, to put it another way, how could that £331,287 have been spent better?

It would have paid for thirteen full-time teaching assistants for a full year, to help young people who are struggling at school.

Or 600 households could have had their council tax waived for three months each when they were struggling financially.

Or it could have been spent on the roads, and 288 potholes could have been filled.

Or it could have paid for three full-time GPs for a whole year, to visit the vulnerable in their own homes, doing one-hour visits to review complex cases.

The painful truth is that I didn't win, but neither did the council, the managers or the community and residents of the area. Because of poor leadership and ineffective HR support, everybody lost.

But it doesn't have to be this way. It may have been slightly ridiculous to give me a head of HR job in my twenties, I was hugely out of my depth and not really experienced enough, but it has given me the opportunity to try everything I could think of and learn, learn, learn. And although this last five years have been painful beyond belief, this time has supercharged my learning. I have been able to apply my thinking, in a much wider field of organisations, and had more freedom in the methods I've used as a freelance consultant than I had in an in house role. HR as it is struggling, both the individuals and function as a whole. It is no one's fault. We can all only use the skills and knowledge that is available to us at the time and do the best we can.

Can you imagine being a medical doctor 300 years ago? With little understanding of basic anatomy, and no idea about viruses or bacteria? Sure, you could do your best, but it is a hell of a lot easier to cure and help ill people with the technology and knowledge that we have now than what existed then.

HR is still learning. It has only really existed for 100 years, and we are still finding our feet. But there are lots of creative HR professionals out there learning, trying new things, learning some more and then creating practices and methods that work better.

It takes time for these ideas to be shared and become mainstream, but they will. And well I'm already working on my next book, that draws together everything I've learnt about how to do HR and how not to do HR, that covers all the amazing things I've learnt and how to apply them, I call this "Beyond HR", it is a system of practices and ideas that I have been collecting and using for years.

I've been sharing this informally for years, but now as an entrepreneur I have the opportunity to share it more widely and in a more organised format. I am currently building several new courses, and when they are ready to BETA test I will need some help to run through these courses to fine tune them, because I totally believe in collaborative learning.

These courses will be advanced courses for HR practitioners and senior managers who have a solid grounding but really want to lean in and develop their skills to the highest possible level.

And as always one of the best bits about these courses (for me as well as everyone else) is that the greatest leaps of learning come when we do it together, bouncing of each other, sharing our ideas and thoughts and fears, feeling supported and nurtured through what is always a difficult and scary process - to learn.

I'm a great believer in mediation. Leadership first, then mediation then case management. If leaders are skilled employee relations issues can often be managed or resolved early on (although this isn't always possible, sometimes leaders are too close to the situation or the employees issues are actually more to do with things going on outside of work, and work issues are a trigger, but not the main issue so it is hard to find a resolution in work). If this doesn't work, mediation is the next step, my friend Pete Colby has a fabulous company that both offers mediation support, but also trains specialists and in-house mediators. This is always the best next step and can resolve almost all situations. But it does require both parties to be willing to come to the table and talk about their situations and sometimes people are unable to do that. Mediation only works when both parties are prepared to genuinely give it a go. In my story, you might remember I attended mediation twice, but David walked out, unable to face me, and NNC were so scared of me they couldn't countenance any outcome that didn't involve a Non-Disclosure Agreement, preferring to try to spend lots of money to destroy me. So sometimes people won't agree to mediation in the first place, or essentially walk out or refuse to be realistic about the outcomes. Pete and I have had many chats about how effective mediation is, and his LinkedIn posts and blogs are an excellent resource for anyone trying to resolve issues early without needing to go to court.

But if none of this works, then case management is the last resort, and that is what I support people to learn to do.

If this issue had been raised by someone other than me, and if I had been supporting ENC to deal with the issue, it would never have gone this badly wrong.

And they could have spent the money they spent fighting me, on more important things.

Chapter 19
Free women are always difficult women

Why is calling a woman "difficult" such a complicated label?

I think Helen Lewis[56] describes it better than I ever could in her article "Fighting the tyranny of 'niceness': why we need difficult women"

"Difficult. It's a word that rests on a knife-edge: when applied to a woman, it can be admiring, fearful, insulting and dismissive, all at once".

So like many people who have had words used as weapons against them, I'm going to lean into the positive, and ignore the insult. I am going to convert them into compliments.

Yes, I'm difficult: I'm difficult, and weird, and even fat, and I'm OK with being all of those things.

I am no longer going to allow those words to be used as weapons, because they are no longer powerful to me. You can use those words about me, but they will not harm me, your daggers will become pink jelly as they fly towards me, easily deflected and of no consequence.

Not easy to do at times, but magical all the same.

Chapter 20
Join the revolution!

If I haven't met you already, I can't wait to, I know we are going to be great friends. We are going to talk late into the night and tell stories and never want it to end...

But this isn't your everyday revolution. I mean it's me, I don't do anything like anyone else does, so why would I create a revolution like everyone else.

This is a revolution of love and forgiveness. There is no place for blame. There is a place for accountability. We will hold those who treat us badly to account. We will no longer sit in the shadows. And we will not do it alone. We are not alone, there are lots of us, and well now you know me....

We are throwing down the shackles of being good girls, we are all becoming free women.

We (and I mean men and women, young and old, Labour and Conservative) will roll our sleeves up and clean up. We may not have made this mess, but we are going to fix it, one bit at a time. And we aren't going to turn into the behaviours we are running from, we are going to create something new.

And we aren't going to exclude those that have made mistakes from helping to create the solutions. In fact, we are going to embrace their involvement, because they have learnt how not to do something, which is always invaluable.

There is one simple rule.

Own your shit.

Fix it, learn from it, move on, and you will be welcomed with open arms, because the future is yours.

Blame and shame and guilt others or hide from what you've done, and well you might just see my angry side, and the angry side of millions like me.

Because

WE

HAVE

HAD

ENOUGH

But do the work, find ways to understand why you did these things, and you will be just as welcome, and I will give you a hug and stand by your side if anyone attacks you.

I am not a man hater, I absolutely adore men ☺. But well, if you underestimate me, and think my kindness and forgiveness are just a sign of weakness, well... go on... see how that turns out for you...

But I can't do this alone.

I don't want to do this alone.

A) It's far more fun with people - like everything, a cold wet Sunday morning can be fun with the right crowd.

B) It isn't about grand gestures, it's not about building statues, or spending millions. We change this one little kindness at a time. If you see someone who is struggling, maybe a stranger in the street seems distressed and a little sad. Walk up to him or her and say "I love your shoes/skirt/hair/book" It doesn't matter what they are wearing, it is just code for, I see you, you are amazing, no matter how shit you think you've done, how terrible your day is, you are good enough and you are not alone, I see you. You are worthy of love; you make a difference in this world. The seventies were ages ago, it's time for a new era of love, only in this one, we have power too...

So join me, join the revolution.

Escape the Good Girl Trap.

Become a free woman (or support the women around you to be free).

I

DARE

YOU!

Tell me your thoughts and stories by scanning the QR code here .....

Chapter 21
My Happy Ending

The tiny flame I rediscovered at the beginning of this story is now a furnace that churns out joy and warmth and ideas. I found happiness, connection, purpose and my sense of fun.

A friend asked me this week how I was and without a hesitation I replied "fabulous".

The journey may have been arduous, but the destination is Magical.

The Employment Genie
Aime Ayrehart

NINJA HR
Helping professionals get a fair deal at work

HR & WORKERS TRADE UNION
Helping each other get a fair deal at work

EMDT
Entrepreneur Mindset Development Tool

The SASS PRENEUR Club

Chapter 22
Thank You's

When your life is full of amazing people, and they are so kind and generous and wonderful, how on earth do you try to do justice to what they mean to you?

Well, I guess the obvious answer is I can't, and any attempt to even try would I think be woefully inadequate. So instead, I will make a more general thank you to everyone who has been there for me over these dark and difficult few years.

So, to everyone who has offered a kindly ear, a friendly smile, a like on a post or a hug: thank you. You will never know just how important these acts of kindness have been to me on tough days.

It might seem like nothing ever hurts me, but that is just because I'm tough, and I'll keep going no matter how much I'm hurting inside. It's not because I'm not hurting.

So, thank you from the bottom of my heart...

But I couldn't do a thank you page without thanking my amazing family.

The biggest thank you goes to my daughters, my parents, my brother and sister (and brother and sister in law) and perhaps somewhat surprisingly my ex husband.

I have always known I was loved and accepted, no matter what I did. That unconditional love comes from my family. And to them I will be eternally grateful.

There are advantages and disadvantages of having a Mum like me. But my eternal gratitude goes to my daughters for seeing the good through the chaos. And thank you for all the hugs and laughter. Whatever happens in my life, you will always be the best bundles of wonderfulness I will ever create (yep I did just make it all about me ☺). Despite the challenges of the last few years, seeing you flourish into amazing young women with your own ideas and approaches has been an absolute joy. I learn so much from you all the time, and I can't wait to see what happens next in your lives.

To Gordon, thank you for being supportive no matter how hard it got, and for being a great partner in life and a fabulous dad to our girls. In an era when not many people truly co-parent and women often take the burden of housework and childcare, I have the upmost respect that you always did not only your fair share, but often more than I did. And still managing to play tennis for GB and save people's lives in the NHS! Whilst our lives are now going on separate tracks, I look forward to long drunken conversations about politics and economics at various family get togethers in the future and seeing you happy in your new life.

To my parents, thank you for giving me the kind of childhood and love that most people can only dream of. I mean obviously you are hugely embarrassing and drive me nuts, but I do actually like hanging out with you, even though it is hard to admit my Mum is cooler than me ☺.

I'd also like to thank Helen Mirren, Emma Thompson, Michelle Obama, Reese Witherspoon, Sandi Toksvig and Idris Elba for all the encouragement you have provided me. Admittedly it was only as figments of my own subconscious, but you are all really cool, and gave fabulous counsel anyway (well except Idris... obviously he was in my dreams for very different reasons!).

And of course, last but very much not least, to Clare. Without whom, in many many ways, this book would never have existed. Thank you for being the friend I needed when I felt I had none.

Chapter 23

A note to anyone who is unhappy about how they have been represented in this book

I have tried to write the story of what happened at ENC and over the last few years of my life as best I can. My memory is good but it isn't perfect. If you feel that I have got something factually wrong, then get in touch. I will have the text of the book updated if it is clear that I have been factually inaccurate.

Some of the comments, however, are not statements of fact, but my opinions. I think it is pretty clear in the book where I'm stating that something is a fact, and where I'm saying something that is my opinion. But again, if you feel this isn't clear enough, then let me know what the phrase is on what page and if I can improve the text, and I agree that it is unclear, then I will update it.

I have also tried to hide the identity of most of the people in this book, if you feel I have talked about you, but that someone can still work out who you are, then apologies. And again, get in touch and let's see if I can improve the wording to hide you better.

Fundamentally I've tried to be fair and kind to both the people in this book, and myself, and if you feel that anything is not quite right, or you aren't happy with something, then get in touch and we can discuss and attempt to find a resolution.

Chapter 24
References

1. The returning officer is the person legally responsible for making sure the election is run properly, it is nearly always a Local Authority Chief Executive, but where there is an election that goes across the boundaries of several local authorities some CEO's act as Deputies.
2. p 1614 of the Employment Tribunal Bundle
3. 7.7 p 1633 Employment Tribunal Bundle
4. 7.3 p 1632 Employment Tribunal Bundle
5. The government Advisory, Conciliation and Arbitration Service. You are not allowed to even go to an Employment Tribunal before you've gone through the ACAS system and they have tried to persuade you not to go to court. An interesting organisation which I got to find out a lot more about when I was invited as part of a tendering process to deal with their own staff issues and I got to go behind the scenes. LINK to ACAS definition of Bullying https://www.acas.org.uk/bullying-at-work
6. https://www.parliament.uk/business/news/2023/october-2023/independent-expert-panel-recommends-suspending-peter-bone-mp-for-bullying-and-sexual-misconduct/
7. https://www.theguardian.com/politics/2023/oct/16/tory-mp-peter-bone-hit-and-abused-staff-member-watchdog-says
8. https://www.nhsemployers.org/publications/identity-checks-standard#:~:text=Undertaking identity checks minimises the,genuine documents to gain employment.
9. https://www.theguardian.com/uk/2003/dec/17/soham.ukcrime2
10. There are certain exceptions to this, Disclosure and Barring Service (DBS) checks are done more frequently to check for criminal convictions, but as with the issue with Ian Huntley, they are only of any use if we have validated the name of the person involved correctly at the beginning. If they are using a fake name then we might never find out who they are or what crimes that they have committed.
11. https://www.gov.uk/government/publications/right-to-work-checks-employers-guide
12. p672 and 6733 of the Employment Tribunal Bundle
13. p608 and 609 of the Employment Tribunal Bundle
14. -
15. p648 of the Employment Tribunal Bundle
16. ENC Housing Needs Assessment Survey Results 2004
17. By the way this doesn't mean that if your boss promises to always let you sit at a certain desk or have a certain office they are legally bound to keep to this rule, it is a little more complicated than this. But be careful about gifts, there is a lovely case about Christmas Turkeys and how these became a contractually required gift...
18. p2432 of the Employment Tribunal Bundle
19. p2590-2594 Employment Tribunal Bundle
20. "Evolution - the Human Story" Dr Alice Roberts
21. https://www.bbc.com/future/article/20191001-dunbars-number-why-we-can-only-maintain-150-relationships#:~:text=Other numbers are nested within,(people you can recognise).
22. https://www.psy.ox.ac.uk/publications/295994
23. https://www.psychologytoday.com/gb/blog/bully-wise/202007/the-pain-of-ostracization-the-bullys-silent-weapon

24. https://health.clevelandclinic.org/good-girl-syndrome/#:~:text=Think about the term "good,Albers explains.
25. https://www.theguardian.com/society/2019/jul/29/northamptonshire-social-services-failing-to-keep-children-safe-says-ofsted#:~:text=Ofsted said its inspection, carried harmful situations for too long.
26. https://www.theguardian.com/society/2018/feb/02/tory-run-council-runs-out-of-money-to-meet-obligations
27. https://www.northamptonchron.co.uk/news/politics/everything-you-need-to-know-about-the-northamptonshire-council-changes-coming-into-force-on-april-1-3150918
28. https://www.northantslive.news/news/northamptonshire-news/battle-over-953-million-disaggregation-8940797
29. https://www.bbc.co.uk/news/uk-england-northamptonshire-36342097
30. https://www.bbc.co.uk/news/uk-england-northamptonshire-48635993
31. https://www.bbc.co.uk/news/uk-england-northamptonshire-55799753
32. https://www.bbc.co.uk/news/uk-england-northamptonshire-44716214
33. https://www.bbc.co.uk/news/uk-england-northamptonshire-53696561
34. https://www.bbc.co.uk/news/uk-england-northamptonshire-37405805
35. https://www.newcastle.gov.uk/services/environment-and-waste/investigations-and-enforcement-policies/being-invited-interview
36. p1646 and 1647 of the Employment Tribunal Bundle
37. https://www.northamptonchron.co.uk/news/former-chief-finance-officer-heavily-criticised-over-delay-of-accounts-at-northampton-borough-council-131017
38. https://www.northantstelegraph.co.uk/news/people/police-called-in-over-east-northants-council-fraud-3553411
39. p2053 of Employment Tribunal Bundle
40. p2257 onwards in the Employment Tribunal Bundle
41. https://www.taxpayersalliance.com/local_authority_spending_on_settlement_agreements
42. https://www.royalnavy.mod.uk/our-organisation/maritime-reserves/royal-naval-reserve/units/president
43. https://en.wikipedia.org/wiki/Stirrup_cup
44. -
45. https://www.vox.com/2016/9/19/12865500/politics-of-pockets-suffragettes-women
46. https://www.gentlemansgazette.com/white-tie-do-dont-dress-code-met-ball
47. https://thedrapers.co.uk/
48. https://www.householddivision.org.uk/ceremonial-events
49. https://www.instagram.com/p/CugpUefMulb/
50. https://www.bbc.co.uk/news/uk-england-shropshire-65481441?fbclid=IwAR2WJULHyxK9M4w0fPhrVUVUiJeJxZ8fXhZyXXaptBRQAb1X43qRyV98XV4
51. There are some exceptions to this - I can't answer direct questions that are asked of you in a disciplinary hearing for example. But I can ask questions, raise issues, write documents and sum up in hearings.
52. These are like work experience, but tend to be done by students already studying law. They are difficult to get, and give an opportunity to get to know a set of barristers, if they go well it might lead to being invited to do a pupillage which is basically the first stage of becoming a barrister after the law degree and being called to the bar)
53. https://www.mindtools.com/a8nu5v5/kotters-8-step-change-model
54. https://www.northantstelegraph.co.uk/news/people/another-east-northants-council-legal-case-looms-over-new-authority-3605972
55. https://www.northantstelegraph.co.uk/news/people/former-east-northants-council-hr-boss-to-claim-unfair-dismissal-at-employment-tribunal-3639270?r=8427
56. https://www.theguardian.com/books/2020/feb/15/feminism-feminists-tyranny-niceness-complexity

Printed in Great Britain
by Amazon

38706993R00145